VAMPIRES, WEREWOLVES AND THINGS THAT GO BUMP IN THE NIGHT

KEN HUDNALL
Omega Press
El Paso, Texas

**VAMPIRES, WEREWOLVES AND THINGS THAT
GO BUMP IN THE NIGHT
COPYRIGHT © 2014 KEN HUDNALL**

OMEGA PRESS

An imprint of Omega Communications Group, Inc.

For information contact:

Omega Press

5823 N. Mesa, #839

El Paso, Texas 79912

Or http://www.kenhudnall.com

FIRST EDITION

Printed in the United States of America

**OTHER WORKS BY THE SAME AUTHOR
UNDER THE NAME KEN HUDNALL
FROM OMEGA PRESS
MANHATTAN CONSPIRACY SERIES**
Blood on the Apple
Capitol Crimes
Angel of Death

THE OCCULT CONNECTION
UFOs, Secret Societies and Ancient Gods
The Hidden Race
Flying Saucers
UFOs and the Supernatural
UFOs and Secret Societies
UFOs and Ancient Gods
Evidence of Alien Contact

DARKNESS
When Darkness Falls
Fear The Darkness

SPIRITS OF THE BORDER
(with Connie Wang)
The History and Mystery of El Paso Del Norte
The History and Mystery of Fort Bliss, Texas

(with Sharon Hudnall)
The History and Mystery of the Rio Grande
The history and Mystery of New Mexico
The History and Mystery of the Lone Star State
The History and Mystery of Arizona
The History and Mystery of Tombstone, AZ
The History and Mystery of Colorado
Echoes of the Past
El Paso: A City of Secrets

Tales From The Nightshift
The History and Mystery of Sin City
The History and Mystery of Concordia
Nautical Ghosts
Haunted Hotels

THE ESTATE SALE MURDERS
Dead Man's Diary

Northwood Conspiracy

No Safe Haven; Homeland Insecurity

Where No Car Has Gone Before

Seventy Years and No Losses: The History of the Sun

Bowl

How Not To Get Published

PUBLISHED BY PAJA BOOKS
The Occult Connection: Unidentified Flying Objects

DEDICATION
As with all of my books, I could not have completed this book if not for my lovely wife, Sharon.

TABLE OF CONTENTS

PART ONE

VAMPIRES

CHAPTER ONE

THE VAMPIRE

This book is about the monsters that haunt our dreams; those incredible creatures that cause the bravest among us to look fearfully over our shoulders. In this section we will look at the vampire, that allegedly immortal creature who lurks in the dark and craves our blood.

Figure 1: The Vampire (1897) from author's collection

According to science, Vampires are merely mythical beings who subsist by feeding on the life essence (generally in the form of blood) of living creatures.

In folklore, vampires often returned from the grave to visit loved ones and caused mischief or deaths in the neighborhoods they had inhabited when they were alive. The newly undead wore burial shrouds and were often described as bloated and of ruddy or dark countenance, markedly different from today's gaunt, pale vampire which dates from the early 1800s.

Figure 2: They come when we sleep from author's collection

Although vampire like entities have been recorded in most cultures from time immemorial, the term vampire was not popularized until the early 18th century, after an influx of vampire superstition into Western Europe from areas where vampire legends were frequent, such as the Balkans and Eastern Europe[1], although local variants were also known by different names, such as Vrykolakas in Greece and Strigoi in Romania.

This increased level of vampire superstition in Europe led to what can only be called mass hysteria (by

[1] Silver & Ursini, *The Vampire Film*, pp. 22-23.

scientists) and in some cases resulted in corpses actually being staked and people being accused of vampirism.

In modern times, however, the vampire is generally held to be a fictitious entity, although belief in similar vampiric creatures such as the Chupacabra still persists in some cultures. Early folkloric belief in vampires has been ascribed to the ignorance of the body's process of decomposition after death and how people in pre-industrial societies tried to rationalize this, creating the figure of the vampire to explain the mysteries of death. Porphyria[2] was

also linked with legends of vampirism in 1985 and received much media exposure, but has since been largely discredited.

Most of us grew up watching Bela Lugosi[3] playing Count Dracula in the late movies. The

Figure 3: Count Dracula used with permission

[2]The porphyrias are a group of rare inherited or acquired disorders of certain enzymes that normally participate in the production of porphyrins and heme. They manifest with either neurological complications or skin problems or occasionally both.

[3] Béla Ferenc Dezső Blaskó, better known as Bela Lugosi, was a Hungarian-American actor, famous for portraying Count Dracula in the original 1931 film and for his roles in various other horror films.

charismatic and sophisticated vampire of modern fiction was born in 1819 with the publication of *The Vampyre* by John Polidori[4]; the story was highly successful and arguably the most influential vampire work of the early 19th century[5].

However, it is Bram Stoker's 1897 novel **Dracula**[6] which is remembered as the quintessential vampire novel and provided the basis of the modern vampire legend. The success of this book spawned a distinctive vampire genre, still popular in the 21st century, with books, films, and television shows. The vampire has since become a dominant figure in the horror genre.

Figure 4: An artist rendition of a supposed Strigoi, author's collection

So now we have seen what science says about the Vampire, however, this author is the host of a nightly radio show that discusses the paranormal. I have had

[4] Polidori, John, *The Vampyre*, CreateSpace Independent Publishing Platform (May 27, 2012)
[5] Silver & Ursini, *The Vampire Film*, pp. 37-38
[6] Stoker, Bram, *Dracula*, Dover Publications (April 18, 2000)

occasion to interview a young lady who claims to be of Gypsy descent. She related that several decades ago, as her family, who lived in Romania at the time, crossed land belonging to Romanian noble families who claimed to be Strigoi, during the time they were on Strigoi land they had to turn over a young female (in this case her aunt) to the landowner who would feed on the "guest" during the period that the family was on the noble's land. According to my guest, there was never any harm done to the captive who reported that she was very well treated while in captivity.

So are Vampires real or merely folk lore or perhaps something in between? After reading the book, you decide.

CHAPTER TWO

WHAT IS A VAMPIRE?

So it would seem that science and those who live in the eastern European areas that are the supposed home

Figure 5: Nosferatu from author's collection

of the Vampires have a different opinion about exactly what these creatures are and how long they have fed off humanity.

The Oxford English Dictionary dates the first appearance of the word vampire in English from 1734, in a travelogue titled *Travels of Three English Gentlemen* published in <u>The Harleian Miscellany</u>[7] in 1745[8]. However, it should be noted that the original article did not actually use the spelling vampire, but used vampyre[9]. Even earlier English language references to the word vampire can be found in the form of vampyre. An example is found in re-telling the famous case of Arnold Paole and Peter Plogojowitz in Serbia, where the *London Journal* of March 11, 1732, describes vampyres in Hungary (actually northern Serbia under direct Austrian rule) as sucking the blood of the living[10].

Vampires had already been discussed in French[11] and German literature. After Austria gained control of northern Serbia and Oltenia with the Treaty of Passarowitz

---

[7] The Harleian Miscellany was a collection of material from the library of the Earl of Oxford collated and edited by Samuel Johnson and William Oldys between 1744 and 1753 on behalf of the publisher Thomas Osborne. Its subtitle was A Collection of Scarce, Curious, And Entertaining Pamphlets And Tracts, as well In Manuscript As In Print, Found In The Late Earl Of Oxford's Library, Interspersed With Historical, Political, And Critical Notes.

[8] J. Simpson, E. Weiner (eds), ed. (1989). "Vampire". Oxford English Dictionary (2nd ed.). Oxford: Clarendon Press.

[9] Johnson, Samuel (Ed.) (1745). The Harleian Miscellany: A collection of scarce, curious, and entertaining pamphlets and tracts, as well in manuscript as in print. Vol. IV. London: T. Osborne. p. 358.

[10] As quoted in The Gentleman's Magazine, May, 1732; Vol. 2, No. 17, pp.750-752 "Political Vampyres."

[11] Vermeir, K. (2012). Vampires as Creatures of the Imagination: Theories of Body, Soul, and Imagination in Early Modern Vampire Tracts (1659–1755). In Y. Haskell (Ed.), Diseases of the Imagination and Imaginary Disease in the Early Modern Period. Turnhout: Brepols Publishers.

in 1718, officials noted the local practice of exhuming bodies and "killing vampires". These reports, prepared between 1725 and 1732, received widespread publicity.

Figure 6: Another version of the Vampire, used with permission

The English term was derived (possibly via French vampyre) from the German Vampir, in turn derived in the early 18th century from the Serbian vampir[12] [13] [14] [15] when Arnold Paole, a purported vampire in Serbia was described during the time when Northern Serbia was part of the Austrian Empire.

The Serbian form has parallels in virtually all Slavic languages: Bulgarian and Macedonian (vampir), Bosnian: lampir, Croatian vampir, Czech and Slovak upír, Polish

---

[12] "Deutsches Wörterbuch von Jacob Grimm und Wilhelm Grimm. 16 Bde. (in 32 Teilbänden). Leipzig: S. Hirzel 1854–1960". Archived from the original on 26 September 2007. Retrieved 2006-06-13.

[13] Jump up ^ "Vampire". Merriam-Webster Online Dictionary. Retrieved 2006-06-13.

[14] (French) "Trésor de la Langue Française informatisé". Retrieved 2006-06-13.

[15] (French) Dauzat, Albert (1938). Dictionnaire étymologique de la langue française. Paris: Librairie Larousse. OCLC 904687.

wąpierz, and (perhaps East Slavic-influenced) upiór, Ukrainian (upyr), Russian (upyr'), Belarusian (upyr), from Old East Slavic (upir'). (Note that many of these languages have also borrowed forms such as "vampir/wampir" subsequently from the West; these are distinct from the original local words for the creature.) The exact etymology is unclear[16]. Among the proposed proto-Slavic forms are ǫpyrъ and ǫpirь[17]. Another, less widespread theory, is that the Slavic languages have borrowed the word from a Turkic term for "witch" (e.g., Tatar ubyr)[18].

An early use of the Old Russian word is in the anti-pagan treatise "*Word of Saint Grigoriy*" (Russian Слово святого Григория), dated variously to the 11th–13th centuries, where pagan worship of upyri is reported[19]. So

---

[16] (Russian) Tokarev, Sergei Aleksandrovich (1982). Mify Narodov Mira. Sovetskaya Entsiklopediya: Moscow. OCLC 7576647. ("Myths of the Peoples of the World"). Upyr'

[17] (Russian) "Russian Etymological Dictionary by Max Vasmer". Retrieved 2006-06-13.

[18] (Bulgarian)Mladenov, Stefan (1941). Etimologičeski i pravopisen rečnik na bălgarskiya knižoven ezik.

[19] Gregory of Narek (Armenian: Գրիգոր Նարեկացի Grigor Narekatsi; 951 – 1003) was an Armenian monk, poet, mystical philosopher, theologian and saint of the Armenian Apostolic Church, born into a family of writers. He was "Armenia's first great poet". He is the author of mystical interpretation on the Song of Songs and numerous poetic writings. His Book of Prayers, also known as "Book of Lamentations", a long mystical poem in 95 sections written around 977 has been translated to many languages. The book, the work of his mature years remains one of the definitive pieces of Armenian literature. He called it his last testament: "its letters like my body, its

clearly, there was enough evidence to convince a number of early reporters that Vampires existed.

In fact, the notion of vampirism has existed for millennia; numerous cultures such as the Mesopotamians, Hebrews, Ancient Greeks, and Romans had tales of demons and spirits that lusted after Human blood and which are considered precursors to modern vampires.

However, despite the occurrence of vampire-like creatures in these ancient civilizations, the folklore for the entity we know today as the vampire originates almost exclusively from early-18th-century southeastern Europe, when verbal traditions of many ethnic groups of the region were recorded and published.

In most cases, vampires are considered to be revenants of evil beings, suicide victims, or witches, but they can also be created by a malevolent spirit possessing a corpse or by a Human being bitten by someone who is already a vampire. Belief in such legends became so pervasive that in some areas it caused mass hysteria and even public executions of people believed to be vampires.

---

message like my soul". Gregory, later a saint of the Armenian Apostolic Church left this world in 1003, but his voice continues to speak to us.

How to Spot a Vampire

Figure 7: Catching the Vampire in his coffin, author's collection

It is difficult to make a single, definitive description of a vampire based on folklore, though there are several elements common to many of the European legends. In spite of their urbane appearance as exemplified by Lugosi's Count Dracula, in folklore Vampires were usually reported as bloated in appearance, and ruddy, purplish, or dark in color; these characteristics were often attributed to the recent drinking of blood.

Indeed, when intrepid vampire hunters would dig up an alleged blood drinker, blood was often seen seeping from the mouth and nose when one was seen in its shroud or coffin and its left eye was often open[20]. It would be clad in the linen shroud it was buried in, and its teeth, hair, and nails may have grown somewhat, though in general fangs were not a feature[21].

---

[20] Barber, Paul, *Vampires, Burial, and Death: Folklore and Reality*, Yale University Press (July 25, 1988)
[21] Ibid

How a Vampire is Created

Figure 8: Russian Orthodox Church, author's collection

The factors that led to the creation of a Vampire were many and varied in original folklore. Many times, especially in the Russian Orthodox Church it was seen as a punishment from God for some transgression.

In Slavic and Chinese traditions, any corpse that was jumped over by an animal, particularly a dog or a cat, was feared to become one of the undead[22]. A body with a

Figure 9: Crossing the River Styx, author's collection

wound that had not been treated with boiling water was also at risk. In Russian folklore, vampires were said to have once been witches or people who had rebelled against the Russian Orthodox Church while they were alive[23].

---

[22] Ibid

Socially, cultural practices often arose that were intended to prevent a recently deceased loved one from turning into an undead revenant. Burying a corpse upside-down was a widespread belief, as was placing earthly objects, such as scythes or sickles[24], near the grave to satisfy any demons entering the body or to appease the dead so that it would not wish to arise from its coffin.

This method resembles the Ancient Greek practice of placing an obolus[25] in the corpse's mouth to pay the toll to cross the River Styx[26] in the underworld; it has been argued that instead, the coin was intended to ward off any evil spirits from entering the body, and this may have influenced later vampire folklore. This tradition persisted in modern Greek folklore about the Vrykolakas[27], in which a

---

[23] Reader's Digest Association (1988). "Vampires Galore!". The Reader's Digest Book of strange stories, amazing facts: stories that are bizarre, unusual, odd, astonishing, incredible ... but true. London: Reader's Digest. pp. 432–433.

[24] Barber, Paul, *Vampires, Burial, and Death: Folklore and Reality*, Yale University Press (July 25, 1988)

[25] A silver coin or unit of weight equal to one sixth of a drachma, formerly used in ancient Greece.

[26] The Styx (/stɪks/; Ancient Greek: Στύξ [stýkʰs], "Hate, Detest") is a river in Greek mythology that formed the boundary between Earth and the Underworld (often called Hades which is also the name of this domain's ruler). The rivers Styx, Phlegethon, Acheron, and Cocytus all converge at the center of the underworld on a great marsh, which is also sometimes called the Styx.

[27] The vrykolakas, is a harmful undead creature in Greek folklore. It has similarities to many different legendary creatures, but is generally equated with the vampire of the folklore of the neighbouring Slavic

Figure 10: Vrykolakas

wax cross and piece of pottery with the inscription "Jesus Christ conquers" were placed on the corpse to prevent the body from becoming a vampire[28]. Other methods of trying to stop the depredations of a vampire commonly practiced in Europe included severing the tendons at the knees of the recently dead or placing poppy seeds, millet, or sand on the ground around the grave site of a presumed vampire; this was intended to keep the vampire occupied all night by counting the fallen grains[29], indicating an association of vampires with arithmomania[30].

---

countries. While the two are very similar, blood-drinking is only marginally associated with the vrykolakas.

[28] Lawson, John Cuthbert (1910). Modern Greek Folklore and Ancient Greek Religion. Cambridge: Cambridge University Press. pp. 405–06.

[29] Barber, Paul, *Vampires, Burial, and Death: Folklore and Reality*, Yale University Press (July 25, 1988)

[30] Arithmomania is a mental disorder that may be seen as an expression of obsessive–compulsive disorder (OCD).[1] Individuals suffering from this disorder have a strong need to count their actions or objects in their surroundings.[2]

Similar stories from Chinese state that if a vampire-like being came across a sack of rice, it would have to count every grain; this is a theme encountered in myths from the Indian subcontinent, as well as in South American tales of witches and other sorts of evil or mischievous spirits or beings[31].

In Albanian folklore, there is dhampir, the son of the karkanxholl or the lugat. If the karkanxholl sleeps with his wife, and she is impregnated with a child, the offspring is called dhampir and has the unique ability to discern the karkanxholl; from this derives the expression the dhampir knows the lugat. The lugat cannot be seen, he can only be killed by the dhampir, who himself is usually the son of a lugat. In different regions, animals can be revenants as lugats; also, living people during their sleep. Dhampiraj is also an Albanian surname[32].

How to Identify a Vampire

Many elaborate rituals were used to identify a vampire. One method of finding a vampire's grave involved leading a virgin boy through a graveyard or church grounds on a virgin stallion—the horse would supposedly balk at

---

[31] Jaramillo Londoño, Agustín (1986) [1967]. Testamento del paisa (7th ed.). Medellín: Susaeta Ediciones.
[32] Gjurmime albanologjike, Folklor dhe etnologji, Vol. 15, pp. 58–148.

the grave in question[33]. Generally a black horse was required, though in Albania it should be white[34]. Holes appearing in the earth over a grave were taken as a sign of vampirism[35].

Corpses thought to be vampires were generally described as having a healthier appearance than expected, plump and showing little or no signs of decomposition[36].

In some cases, when suspected graves were opened, villagers even described the corpse as having fresh blood from a victim all over its face[37]. Evidence that a vampire was active in a given locality included death of cattle, sheep, relatives or neighbors. Folkloric vampires could also make their presence felt by engaging in minor poltergeist-like activity, such as hurling stones on roofs or moving household objects[38], and pressing on people in their sleep.

[33] Reader's Digest Association (1988). "Vampires Galore!". The Reader's Digest Book of strange stories, amazing facts: stories that are bizarre, unusual, odd, astonishing, incredible ... but true. London: Reader's Digest. pp. 432–433.

[34] Barber, Paul, Vampires, Burial, and Death: Folklore and Reality, Yale University Press (July 25, 1988)

[35] Ibid

[36] Ibid

[37] Ibid

[38] Ibid

CHAPTER THREE
HOW TO DEAL WITH A VAMPIRE

How to Protect Yourself Against a Vampire

Whether or not the vampire was a real threat to Humans, a large body of literature appeared that discussed how to defend against the attacks of these deadly creatures. Some of these methods spoke of religious ceremonies or religious relics, other about various charms that would protect the user from the attack of these undead creatures.

Apotropaics

Apotropaics, items able to ward off revenants, are common in a lot of vampire folklore. Garlic is a common example[39] of such protection. It is a branch of wild rose and hawthorn plant that is said to harm vampires. In Europe, it is said that sprinkling mustard seeds on the roof of a house

---

[39] Barber, Paul, *Vampires, Burial, and Death: Folklore and Reality*, Yale University Press (July 25, 1988)

was said to keep them away[40]. Other apotropaics include sacred items, for example a crucifix, rosary, or holy water.

Vampires are said to be unable to walk on consecrated ground, such as that of churches or temples, or cross running water. Although not traditionally regarded as an apotropaic, mirrors have been used to ward off vampires when placed, facing outwards, on a door (in some cultures, vampires do not have a reflection and sometimes do not cast a shadow, perhaps as a manifestation of the vampire's lack of a soul)[41]. This attribute, although not universal (the Greek Vrykolakas/tympanios was capable of both reflection and shadow), was used by Bram Stoker in Dracula and has remained popular with subsequent authors and filmmakers.

Some traditions also hold that a vampire cannot enter a house unless invited by the owner, although after the first invitation they can come and go as they please. Though folkloric vampires were believed to be more active at night, they were not generally considered vulnerable to sunlight.

---

[40] Mappin, Jenni (2003). *Didjaknow: Truly Amazing & Crazy Facts About... Everything*. Australia: Pancake
[41] Spence, Lewis (1960). *An Encyclopaedia of Occultism*. New Hyde Parks: University Books

Methods of Destruction

For every enemy there has to be a way to destroy it. Methods of destroying suspected vampires varied, with staking the most commonly cited method, particularly in southern Slavic cultures[42]. Ash was the preferred wood in Russia and the Baltic States[43], or hawthorn in Serbia[44], with a record of oak in Silesia. Potential vampires were most

often staked through the heart, though the mouth was targeted in Russia and northern Germany and the stomach in north-eastern Serbia. Piercing the skin of the chest was a way of "deflating" the

Figure 11: A stake through the heart was considered effective, used with permission

bloated vampire; this is similar to the act of burying sharp objects, such as sickles, in with the corpse, so that they may

---

[42] Barber, Paul, *Vampires, Burial, and Death: Folklore and Reality*, Yale University Press (July 25, 1988)

[43] (German) Alseikaite-Gimbutiene, Marija (1946). Die Bestattung in Litauen in der vorgeschichtlichen Zeit. Tübingen. OCLC 1059867. (thesis).

[44] Vukanović, T.P. (1959). "The Vampire". Journal of the Gypsy Lore Society 38: 111–18.

penetrate the skin if the body bloats sufficiently while transforming into a revenant[45]. Decapitation was the preferred method in German and western Slavic areas, with the head buried between the feet, behind the buttocks or away from the body[46]. This act was seen as a way of hastening the departure of the soul, which in some cultures, was said to linger in the corpse.

Figure 12: According to legend, wooden stakes had many uses

The vampire's head, body, or clothes could also be spiked and pinned to the earth to prevent rising[47]. Romani drove steel or iron needles into a corpse's heart and placed bits of steel in the mouth, over the eyes, ears and between the fingers at the time of burial. They also placed hawthorn in the corpse's sock or drove a hawthorn stake through the legs.

It is clear that in ancient times, it was felt better to keep the Vampire from rising than it was to try and combat

---

[45] Barber, Paul, *Vampires, Burial, and Death: Folklore and Reality*, Yale University Press (July 25, 1988)
[46] Ibid
[47] Ibid

the Vampire once it has risen to walk the earth once more. A Vampire still in its coffin was considered to be more vulnerable than once who was walking in all of its glory.

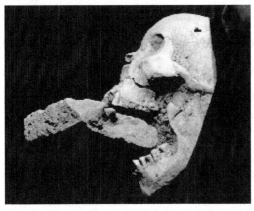

Figure 13: Skull with something placed in its mouth, author's collection

In a 16th-century burial near Venice, a brick forced into the mouth of a female corpse has been interpreted as a vampire-slaying ritual by the archaeologists who discovered it in 2006. Further measures included pouring boiling water over the grave or complete incineration of the [48]body. In the Balkans, a vampire could also be killed by being shot or drowned, by repeating the funeral service, by sprinkling holy water on the body, or by exorcism. In Romania, garlic could be placed in the mouth, and as recently as the 19th century, the precaution of shooting a bullet through the coffin was taken. For resistant cases, the body was dismembered and the pieces burned, mixed with water, and administered to

---

48

family members as a cure. In Saxon regions of Germany, a lemon was placed in the mouth of suspected vampires.

It is also worth mentioning that in Bulgaria, over 100 skeletons with metal objects, such as plough bits, embedded in the torso have been discovered which would seem to indicate that perhaps there was a tremendous fear of Vampires even there..

Ancient Beliefs

Tales of supernatural beings consuming the blood or flesh of the living have been found in nearly every culture around the world for many centuries[49]. Today, we would associate these entities with vampires, but in ancient times, the term vampire did not exist; blood drinking and similar activities were attributed to demons or spirits who would eat flesh and drink blood; even the Devil was considered synonymous with the vampire. Almost every nation has associated blood drinking with some kind of revenant or demon, or in some cases a deity. In India, for example, tales of vetālas, ghoul-like beings that inhabit corpses, have been compiled in the Baitāl Pacīsī; a prominent story in the Kathāsaritsāgara tells of King Vikramāditya and his nightly quests to capture an elusive

---

[49] McNally, Raymond T.; Florescu, Radu. (1994). *In Search of Dracula*. Houghton Mifflin. p. 117.

one[50]. Piśāca, the returned spirits of evil-doers or those who died insane, also bear vampiric attributes[51].

The Persians were one of the first civilizations to publicize tales of blood-drinking demons: creatures attempting to drink blood from men were depicted on excavated pottery shards[52]. Ancient Babylonia and Assyria had tales of the mythical Lilitu[53], synonymous with and giving rise to Lilith[54] and her daughters the Lilu from Hebrew demonology. Lilitu was considered a demon and was often depicted as subsisting on the blood of babies[55]. Estries[56], female shape changing, blood drinking demons, were said to roam the night among the population, seeking victims. According to Sefer Hasidim, Estries were creatures

---

[50] Burton, Sir Richard R. (1893) [1870]. *Vikram and The Vampire:Classic Hindu Tales of Adventure, Magic, and Romance.* London: Tylston and Edwards. ISBN 0-89281-475-6. Retrieved 2007-09-28. Gramercy; 2nd edition (August 1, 2000)

[51] Bunson, Matthew, *The Vampire Encyclopedia,* Gramercy; 2nd edition (August 1, 2000)

[52] Marigny, Jean, *Vampires: The World of the Undead,* Thames & Hudson, Limited, 1994

[53] Hurwitz, Seigmund, *Lilith the First Eve,* Daimon Verlag; 3rd Revised edition edition (August 5, 2009)

[54] Lilith is a Hebrew name for a figure in Jewish mythology, developed earliest in the Babylonian Talmud, who is generally thought to be in part derived from a class of female demons Līlītu in Mesopotamian texts of Assyria and Babylonia.

[55] Hurwitz, Seigmund, *Lilith the First Eve*, Daimon Verlag; 3rd Revised edition edition (August 5, 2009)

[56] Estries are female vampires of Jewish folklore that were believed to prey on Hebrew citizens, particularly men. The name derives from the French strix, a term for a night owl.

created in the twilight hours before God rested[57]. An injured Estrie could be healed by eating bread and salt given her by her attacker.

Figure 14: A relief of Lilith, author's collection

Ancient Greek and Roman mythology described the Empusae[58], the Lamia[59], and the striges. Over time the first two terms became general words to describe witches and demons respectively. Empusa was the daughter of the goddess Hecate and was described as a demonic, bronze-footed creature. She feasted on blood by transforming into a young woman and seduced men as they slept before drinking their blood[60].

The Lamia preyed on young children in their beds at night, sucking their blood, as did the gelloudes or

[57] Shael, Rabbi (1 June 2009). "Rabbi Shael Speaks...Tachles: Vampires, Einstein and Jewish Folklore". Shaelsiegel.blogspot.com. Retrieved 2010-12-05.

[58] Graves, Robert (1990) [1955]. "The Empusae". The Greek Myths. London: Penguin. pp. 189–90.

[59] Graves, Robert, "Lamia", in Greek Myths, pp. 205–206.

[60] *Graves, Robert (1990) [1955]. "The Empusae". The Greek Myths. London: Penguin. pp. 189–90.*

Gello[61]. Like the Lamia, the striges feasted on children, but also preyed on young men. They were described as having the bodies of crows or birds in general, and were later

incorporated into Roman mythology as strix, a kind of nocturnal bird that fed on human flesh and blood[62].

Figure 15: Lamia

[61] Graves, Robert, "Lamia", in Greek Myths, pp. 205–206.
[62] Oliphant, Samuel Grant (1 January 1913). "The Story of the Strix: Ancient". Transactions and Proceedings of the American Philological Association 44: 133–49. doi:10.2307/282549.

CHAPTER FOUR

THE VAMPIRE IN MEDIEVAL TIMES

While stories of the undead and creatures that subsisted on the blood of man date from the earliest periods of history, many of the myths surrounding vampires originated during the medieval period. The 12th-century English historians and chroniclers Walter Map and William of Newburgh recorded accounts of revenants[63], though records in English legends of vampiric beings after this date are scant[64]. The Old Norse draugr is another medieval example of an undead creature with similarities to vampires[65].

Vampires proper originate in folklore widely reported from Eastern Europe in the late 17th and 18th centuries. These tales formed the basis of the vampire

---

[63] William of Newburgh; Paul Halsall (2000). "Book 5, Chapter 22–24". Historia rerum Anglicarum. Fordham University. Retrieved 2007-10-16.

[64] Jones, Stephen, *The Mammoth Book of Vampires*, Running Press (May 20, 2004)

[65] Ármann Jakobsson (2009). "*The Fearless Vampire Killers: A Note about the Icelandic Draugr and Demonic Contamination in Grettis Saga*". Folklore 120: 307–316; p. 309.

legend that later entered Germany and England, where they were subsequently embellished and popularized. One of the earliest recordings of vampire activity came from the region of Istria in modern Croatia, in 1672[66].

Local reports cited the local vampire Jure Grando of the village Khring near Tinjan as the cause of panic among the villagers[67]. A former peasant, Jure died in 1656; however, local villagers claimed he returned from the dead and began drinking blood from the people and sexually harassing his widow. The village leader ordered a stake to be driven through his heart, but when the method failed to kill him, he was subsequently beheaded with better results[68]. That was the first case in history that a real person had been described as a vampire.

During the 18th century, there was a frenzy of vampire sightings in Eastern Europe, with frequent stakings and grave diggings to identify and kill the potential

---

[66] Klinger, Leslie (2008). "Dracula's Family Tree". The New Annotated Dracula. New York: W.W. Norton & Company, Inc. p. 570.

[67] Pile, Steve (2005). "Dracula's Family Tree". Real cities: modernity, space and the phantasmagorias of city life. London: Sage Publications Ltd. p. 570.

[68] Caron, Richard (2001). "Dracula's Family Tree". Ésotérisme, gnoses & imaginaire symbolique: mélanges offerts à Antoine Faivre. Belgium: Peteers, Bondgenotenlaan 153. p. 598. .

revenants; even government officials engaged in the hunting and staking of vampires[69].

Despite being called the Age of Enlightenment, during which most folkloric legends were quelled, the belief in vampires increased dramatically, resulting in a mass hysteria throughout most of Europe. The panic began with an outbreak of alleged vampire attacks in East Prussia in 1721 and in the Habsburg Monarchy from 1725 to 1734, which spread to other localities.

Two famous vampire cases, the first to be officially recorded, involved the corpses of Peter Plogojowitz and Arnold Paole from Serbia. Plogojowitz was reported to have died at the age of 62, but allegedly returned after his death asking his son for food. When the son refused, he was found dead the following day. Plogojowitz supposedly returned and attacked some neighbors who died from loss of blood[70].

In the second case, Paole, an ex-soldier turned farmer who allegedly was attacked by a vampire years before, died while haying. After his death, people began to die in the

[69] Barber, Paul, *Vampires, Burial, and Death: Folklore and Reality*, Yale University Press (July 25, 1988)
[70] Ibid

surrounding area and it was widely believed that Paole had returned to prey on the neighbors[71].

Another famous Serbian legend involving vampires concentrates around a certain Sava Savanović living in a watermill and killing and drinking blood from millers. The character was later used in a story written by Serbian writer Milovan Glišić and in the Yugoslav 1973 horror film Leptirica inspired by the story.

The two incidents were well-documented: government officials examined the bodies, wrote case reports, and published books throughout Europe[72]. The hysteria, commonly referred to as the "18th-Century Vampire Controversy", raged for a generation. The problem was exacerbated by rural epidemics of so-claimed vampire attacks, undoubtedly caused by the higher amount of superstition that was present in village communities, with locals digging up bodies and in some cases, staking them. Although many scholars reported during this period that vampires did not exist, and attributed reports to premature burial or rabies, superstitious belief increased. Dom Augustine Calmet, a well-respected French theologian and scholar, put together a comprehensive

---

[71] Ibid
[72] Ibid

treatise in 1746, which was ambiguous concerning the existence of vampires. Calmet amassed reports of vampire incidents; numerous readers, including both a critical Voltaire and supportive demonologists, interpreted the treatise as claiming that vampires existed[73]. In his *Philosophical Dictionary*, Voltaire wrote[74]:

> *These vampires were corpses, who went out of their graves at night to suck the blood of the living, either at their throats or stomachs, after which they returned to their cemeteries. The persons so sucked waned, grew pale, and fell into consumption; while the sucking corpses grew fat, got rosy, and enjoyed an excellent appetite. It was in Poland, Hungary, Silesia, Moravia, Austria, and Lorraine, that the dead made this good cheer.*

The controversy only ceased when Empress Maria Theresa of Austria sent her personal physician, Gerard van Swieten, to investigate the claims of vampiric entities. He concluded that vampires did not exist and the Empress passed laws prohibiting the opening of graves and desecration of bodies, sounding the end of the vampire

---

[73] Hoyt, Olga Grunhzit, *Lust for Blood*, Rowman & Littlefield Publishers, Inc., 1990
[74] Voltaire (1984) [1764]. Philosophical Dictionary. Penguin.

epidemics. Despite this condemnation, the vampire lived on in artistic works, local superstition and many said in reality.

CHAPTER FIVE

DO VAMPIRES REALLY EXIST

The problem of the vampire can be very simply stated; any rational person will agree that the notion that vampires actually exist has to be based on pure superstition. Surely there is some more rational, simpler and sensible explanation.

The problem is that there are a number of early accounts written with such an air of authority that it is difficult to dismiss them as pure fantasy. One prime example is an eighteenth century report about an undead Serbian[75] that is signed by no less than five Austrian Officers, three of them were doctors. All five had many years of experience and were not easily frightened or misled.

According to their report:

---

[75] This report was entitled *Visum et Repertum* (Seen and Discovered).

After it had been reported in the village of Medvegia, near Belgrade, that so-called vampires had killed some people by sucking their blood, I was by high

decree of a local Honorable Supreme Command, sent there to investigate the matter thoroughly. What I learned was as follows:

About five years ago, a local haiduk called Arnod Paole broke his neck in a fall from a

Figure 16: Emperor Charles VI of Austria

hay wagon. In 20 or 30 days after his

death, some people complained that they were being bothered by this same Arnod Paole; and in fact four people were killed by him. In order to end this evil, they dug up Arnod Paole 40 days after his death—on the order of their Hadnack (a bureaucrat) who had been present at such events before; and they found that he was quite complete and undecayed, and that fresh blood had flowed from his eyes, nose, mouth and ears; that the shirt, the covering and the coffin were completely bloody; that the old nails on his hands and feet, along with the skin, had fallen off, and that new ones had grown. And since they saw from this that he was a true vampire, they drove a stake through his heart - - according to their custom—whereupon he gave an audible groan and bled copiously. Thereupon they burned the body to ashes the same day and thew these into the grave . . . .these same people also say that all of those who have been tormented and killed by vampires must themselves become vampires.

Signed: L.S. Johannes Fluchinger, Regimental Medical Officer of the Foot Regiment of the Honorable B. Furstenbusch.

L.S. J. H. Siegel, Medical Official of the Honorable Morall Regiment.

L.S. Johann Friedricj Baumgarten, Medical officer of the Foot Regiment of the Honorable B. Furstenbusch.

You might be tempted to ignore this as merely peasant superstition, but this is not a secondhand tale and the three doctors were officers in the army of Charles VI, Emperor of Austria. Certainly having fought the Turks from 1714 to 1718, these doctors were very familiar with corpses.

Of course there might be skeptics who say this story comes from so far in the past that it carries little, if any weight, in these modern times. So therefore, let us look at some more modern examples of possible vampires found in their graves.

Recent Discoveries [76]

The mythology of vampires is well-known throughout the world. Most countries have some variation on the vampire legend. Each of these countries also have remarkably similar ways in which vampires can be dispatched, or at least prevented from rising from the grave to plague the living. Modern science has usually dismissed these tales as folklore; however, recent evidence has emerged showing that our ancestors did indeed take these stories seriously.

Over the past few decades, an increasing number of medieval burials have been excavated showing incredible brutality performed on the corpses that exactly matches the methods folklore said must be used to keep a vampire safely in its grave. And these graves are not only being found in the vampire's traditional home of Eastern Europe

---

[76]http://listverse.com/2013/04/04/8-recently-discovered-medieval vampire-burials/

and the Balkans, but in Western Europe too. Here are some of the best-attested cases of medieval vampire burials.

Prostejov, Slovakia

Figure 17: Holy Trinity Church, Prostejov, Solvakia

In 1991, an archaeological investigation of the ancient Church of the Holy Trinity in Prostejov discovered a long hidden crypt burial site secreted in the presbytery.

The body had been buried in a coffin reinforced with iron bars, held to be one method of keeping a vampire buried, since vampires allegedly could not tolerate the touch of iron. In addition, stones had been placed on the victim's legs, and the torso severed from the legs. The find has been dated to the 16th century.

The burial is considered somewhat unusual because of its location in a church, but it has been argued that the extra sanctity of the church may have been thought by those who buried the victim to have been more likely to have kept the corpse in its grave.

Drawsko, Poland

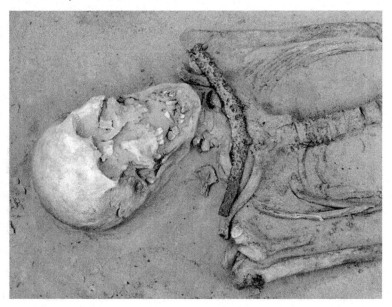

Figure 18: Grave of an alleged vampire

In 2009, at Drawsko in Poland, an archaeological investigation of a medieval cemetery turned up something quite unexpected. Three graves were discovered in which the bodies had been subjected to very unusual treatment post-mortem. Two bodies of middle-aged adults had iron sickles placed on their throats. The body of a younger adult had been tied up and had a heavy stone placed upon his throat. This is in keeping with folklore, traditionally sharp iron implements being held to be anathema to vampires, hence the placement of the sickles as a measure to ensure that the alleged vampire would not rise again. Another method of keeping a suspected vampire in their grave was believed to be the placement of heavy weights upon the body, and the positioning of heavy stones upon bodies has been found in a number of vampire burials. The cemetery has not been fully excavated and archaeologists expect to find similar burials in future years.

Lesbos, Greece

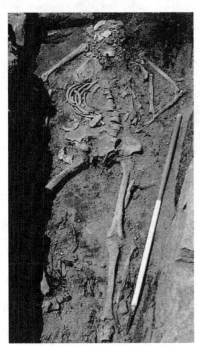

Figure 19: Alleged Vampire

In 1994, on the Greek island of Lesbos, near the city of Mytilene, archaeologists investigating an old Turkish cemetery found a medieval skeleton buried in a crypt hollowed out of an ancient city wall. This was not an unusual discovery; however, the post-mortem treatment of this body was very much unexpected. The corpse had been literally nailed down in its grave, with heavy iron spikes driven through the neck, pelvis and ankle. The use of iron and the practice of staking down a corpse are both well-attested in vampire folklore. The body was almost certainly that of a Muslim, believed to be the first time a corpse of a person other than a Christian had been found treated in this fashion.

Celakovice, Czech Republic

Figure 20: Vampire's grave

In the early 1990s, archaeologists found what is believed to be the first vampires' graveyard—an entire cemetery of vampire burials. In Celakovice, about 30 kilometers north of Prague, 14 graves have been excavated so far with metal spikes driven through their bodies or heavy stones placed upon them. The graves are believed to date from the 11th or 12th century. Most of the victims were young adults, of both sexes. It appears that the victims all died at around the same time, possibly in an epidemic, but it is unclear why the villagers thought these individuals were at risk of becoming vampires.

Sozopol, Bulgaria

Figure 21: Vampires are everywhere

One of the most well publicized cases of recent years, as a Google search will quickly show. Bulgaria is no stranger to vampire burials. More than 100 have been discovered in the past century, but the bulk of those were in remote rural areas. Sozopol is one of Bulgaria's most popular Black Sea tourist resorts, so the discovery of two skeletons with iron spikes jammed through their bodies caused a sensation. The bodies are believed to about 700 years old, and were located buried near a former monastery.

Archaeologists have confirmed that this practice was common in Bulgaria up until the 20th century, and Bulgaria subsequently has become the center of interest for those studying vampire burials.

Venice, Italy

Figure 22: Mouth filled skeleton

As has already been noted, the discovery of vampire burials has been common in the Balkans and Eastern Europe, the heartland of vampire mythology. However, until recently, they were unknown in Western Europe. This is now changing, as archaeological examination of medieval cemeteries in the West is starting to reveal that people here were just as afraid of the dead returning to plague the living.

A well-publicized discovery in 2006 on the island of Lazaretto Nuovo near Venice confirmed that Italy had its own vampire burials. The skeleton of a woman dating from the 16th century was discovered in a cemetery of plague victims. She had a large brick rammed into her mouth prior to burial. This is in keeping with medieval folklore, which held that vampires literally chewed their way out of their burial shrouds, so preventing them from doing this was seen as an effective way of stopping them rising from the grave.

Kilteasheen, Ireland

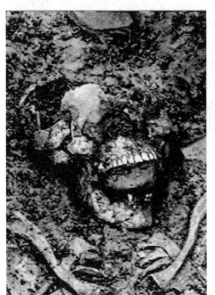

The vampire burial phenomenon struck even deeper into the West with the discovery of two skeletons at Kilteasheen in Ireland between 2005 and 2009. Officially described as "deviant" burials, the skeletons of a middle-aged man and a man in his

Figure 23: Irish Vampire

twenties were discovered lying side by side with rocks rammed into their mouths. The discovery caused a sensation in Ireland and the UK and became the subject of a TV documentary released in 2011.

It has been argued that the victims may have been considered plague-carriers rather than true vampires, because their early burial in the 8th century predates vampire legends in Europe, however, the vampire burial tag has since well and truly stuck in the public consciousness.

Southwell, UK

Figure 24: British Vampires

If complacent Britons had thought their ancestors were far too sophisticated to be taken in by vampire legends as primitive peasants in Eastern Europe had been, they were in for a shock. It was revealed in 2010 that a deviant burial had been found in the Nottinghamshire town of Southwell in 1959, attracting much publicity in the British media.

A long-lost archaeological report compiled during construction of a new school detailed the discovery of a skeleton dating from between A.D. 550 and 700 with metal spikes jammed through heart, shoulders and ankles. The placement of a spike through the heart in particular attracted public interest because of its long association with vampires in myth and legend.

Archaeologists have in fact thrown cold water over the idea that the man was considered a vampire because this particular burial predates vampire legends in Europe, but the idea has seized the public imagination and inspired new research into vampirism in Britain. However, it must be kept in mind that most archeology is supposition. After all, if it walks, like a duck and quakes like a duck it is probably not a squirrel.

CHAPTER SIX

NON-EUROPEAN VAMPIRES

It should be kept in mind that Europe is not the only place where stories of vampires are told. In fact it would be hard to find a location where there are not stories of blood sucking monsters. In that vein, so to speak, let's look at some examples.

Africa

To the African people, vampires exist because they are a class of people who are able to defy death and exert a malignant influence from the

Figure 25: One type of African Vampire, author's collection

grave. African vampires were often people who died in defiance of the community or from suicide.

There are many different types of vampires within African folklore to include Obayifo, Tikoloshe, Adze, Asanbosam, Sasabonsam, Impundulu, and Ramanga. Various regions of Africa have folkloric tales of beings with vampiric abilities: in West Africa the Ashanti people tell of the iron-toothed and tree-dwelling Asanbosam[77] [78], and the Ewe people of the Adze, which can take the form of a firefly and hunts children[79].

The Adze is a vampire creature found in the legends of the Ewe people of Southern Togo. The Adze commonly took the form of a firefly. If caught, the firefly would turn into a quasi-human form with a hunchback, sharp talons, and jet-black skin.

---

[77] Bunson, Matthew, *The Vampire Encyclopedia*, Gramercy; 2nd edition (August 1, 2000)

[78] The Asanbosam is an African vampire found amongst the people of Ghana and Togo. The Asanbosam lives in the trees and forests, feeding mainly on those who wander through its domain.
The vampire waits quietly in the trees, hanging by their curved, hook-like feet, and pounce on its unsuspecting prey. They rip out the throats with their teeth that are made of iron

[79] Bunson, Matthew, *The Vampire Encyclopedia*, Gramercy; 2nd edition (August 1, 2000)

Once in the quasi-human form, the African vampire would kill its victim, drink their blood, and eat the heart and liver. The Adze found children a favorite to feed from.

In some cases, they may feed on palm oil and coconut water, and will often raid a village's supply. These food items are not enough to supply life to the firefly vampire. They will become weak if they do not feed on children. If the Adze is deterred from feeding from long periods of time, it may go on a feeding frenzy for blood; in these cases, the victims will become infected with a deadly disease. The insect vampire will land on the lips and suck blood through an elephant-like truck, which is no wonder why disease of the area are often blamed on insects.

The creature does not have to kill, and in some cases, only takes enough blood to survive without taking the liver and heart.

With enough strength, the Adze can possess a human and become a living vampire, but if captured, it will revert to its human form. A sorcerer is the Adze's favorite to possess, as it obtains the sorcerer's magic, but once captured, the magic is lost and will revert back to human form.

The Adze can only be defeated if caught, but catching them is the trick. There is no way to be protected from the vampire spirit. The Ewe people believed that the best and safest manner to catching and destroying the Adze vampire was to trap them with coconut water and palm oil. If the Adze spirit is captured, the spirit is generally tortured to a slow and painful death.

The Eastern Cape region has the Impundulu, which can take the form of a large taloned bird and can summon thunder and lightning.

The Impundulu vampire is a witch's servant from the Eastern Cape region of Africa. It is found in legends of the

Figure 26: Impundulu

Pondo, the Zulu, and the Xhosa.

The vampire is usually owned by a female and is later passed to the witch's daughter. The witch that controlled the Impundulu vampire made sure that the creature was always fed well in order to avoid the creature turning on her.

If the Impundulu wasn't handed down, it is considered an ownerless monster that will cause chaos.

The African vampire has an insatiable appetite and love for blood and sex. They feed on humans and cattle. It wasn't uncommon for the Impundulu vampire to kill an entire family or herd of cattle, sucking the blood form every victim. The Impundulu would feed on the blood and pain of its victim.

If the African vampire didn't kill them, a wasting disease caused by the vampire would, as the feeding would leave you with a bad cough and infertility.

The different between the Impundulu vampire and the other African vampires is that the Impundulu took the shape of an attractive man instead of an animal creature. Some legends say that the witch and the Impundulu become lovers. In some legends, the Impundulu was seen as a bird creature.

The Betsileo people of Madagascar tell of the Ramanga, an outlaw or living vampire who

Figure 27: the Ramanga, author's collection

drinks the blood and eats the nail clippings of nobles.

The Americas

It is interesting to note that there are even blood sucking monsters to be found in the New World. Of course, as is true with most things, the American bloodsuckers are somewhat different from those in the old world.

Figure 28: Loogaroo, used with permission of the artist

The Loogaroo[80] is an example of how a vampire belief can result from a combination of beliefs, here a

---

[80] The Loogaroo is a monster found in Caribbean mythology. Oddly enough, its name is pronounced the same as "loup-garou", French for "werewolf", despite having nothing in common with werecreatures.

According to the myth, the Loogaroo is an old woman who is said to be in league with The Devil. She will have magical abilities only if she gives the Devil blood every night. She tries to give him blood of other creatures, or else he will take her own blood, causing her to die.

mixture of French and African Vodu or voodoo. The term Loogaroo possibly comes from the French loup-garou (meaning "werewolf") and is common in the culture of Mauritius. However, the stories of the Loogaroo are widespread through the Caribbean Islands and Louisiana in the United States[81].

Similar female monsters are the Soucouyant of Trinidad, who lives by day as an old woman at the end of a village. By night, she strips off her wrinkled skin, which she puts in a mortar, following which she flies in the shape of a fireball through the darkness, looking for a victim. Still a fireball, the Soucouyant enters the home of her victim through cracks and crevices, like keyholes.

The Loogaroo can leave its own skin (usually under a "Devil Tree," a silk cotton tree) and turn into a flame or blue ball of bright light that haunts the night searching for blood to meet the terms of her deal. After she has collected enough blood she can return to her skin and retake human form.

This creature is apparently compulsive and must stop to count grains of sand spread upon the ground. So, a defense against her was to leave a pile of rice or sand near your front door. Hopefully, the creature would take so long to count it all that the sun would eventually return with the coming of morning. By that time the Loogaroo would have to return to her skin without making an attack. In some tales of the Loogaroo, her skin can be taken away from the Devil Tree so that she cannot find it when she returns.

[81] Bunson, Matthew, *The Vampire Encyclopedia*, Gramercy; 2nd edition (August 1, 2000)

Soucouyants suck people's blood from their arms, legs and soft parts while they sleep[82]. If the Soucouyant draws too much blood, it is believed that the victim will either die and become a Soucouyant or perish entirely, leaving her killer to assume her skin. The Soucouyant practices witchcraft, voodoo, and black magic. Soucouyants trade their victims' blood for evil powers with Bazil, the demon who resides in the silk cotton tree[83].

To expose a Soucouyant, one should heap rice around the house or at the village cross roads as the creature will be obligated to gather every grain, grain by grain (a herculean task to do before dawn) so that she can be caught in the act[84]. To destroy her, coarse salt must be placed in the mortar containing her skin so she perishes, unable to put the skin back on. Belief in Soucouyants is still preserved to an extent in some Caribbean islands, including Dominica, St. Lucia, Haiti, and Trinidad[85]. The skin of the Soucouyant is considered valuable, and is used when practicing black magic.

---

[82] The Heritage Library via the Trinidad Guardian
[83] Ibid
[84] Ibid
[85] Maberry, Jonathan (September 1, 2006). *Vampire Universe: The Dark World of Supernatural Beings That Haunt Us*, Hunt .... Citadel. p. 203.

In Columbia there is the Tunda and Patasola, while the Mapuche of southern Chile have the bloodsucking snake known as the Peuchen[86]. Aloe Vera hung backwards behind or near a door was thought to ward off vampiric beings in South American superstition[87]. Aztec mythology described tales of the Cihuateteo, skeletal-faced spirits of those who died in childbirth who stole children and entered into sexual liaisons with the living, driving them mad[88].

During the late 18th and 19th centuries the belief in vampires was widespread in parts of New England, particularly in Rhode Island and Eastern Connecticut. There are many documented cases of families disinterring loved ones and removing their hearts in the belief that the deceased was a vampire who was responsible for sickness and death in the family, although the term "vampire" was never actually used to describe the deceased. The deadly disease tuberculosis, or "consumption" as it was known at the time, was believed to be caused by nightly visitations

[86] (Spanish) Martinez Vilches, Oscar (1992). Chiloe Misterioso: Turismo, Mitologia Chilota, leyendas. Chile: Ediciones de la Voz de Chiloe. p. 179.

[87] (Spanish) Jaramillo Londoño, Agustín (1986) [1967]. Testamento del paisa (7th ed.). Medellín: Susaeta Ediciones.

[88] Reader's Digest Association (1988). "Vampires Galore!". The Reader's Digest Book of strange stories, amazing facts: stories that are bizarre, unusual, odd, astonishing, incredible ... but true. London: Reader's Digest. pp. 432–433.

on the part of a dead family member who had died of consumption themselves[89].

The most famous, and most recently recorded, case of suspected vampirism is that of nineteen-year-old Mercy Brown, who died in Exeter, Rhode Island in 1892. Her father, assisted by the family physician, removed her from her tomb two months after her death, cut out her heart and burned it to ashes[90].

Asia

Rooted in older folklore, the modern belief in vampires spread throughout Asia with tales of ghoulish entities from the mainland, to stories of vampiric beings from the islands of Southeast Asia.

South Asia also developed other vampiric legends. The Bhūta or Prét is the soul of a man who died an untimely death. It wanders around animating dead bodies at night, attacking the living much like a ghoul[91]. In northern India, there is the BrahmarākŞhasa, a vampire-like creature with a head encircled by intestines and a skull from which it drank blood. The figure of the Vetala who appears in

---

[89] Bunson, Matthew, *The Vampire Encyclopedia*, Gramercy; 2nd edition (August 1, 2000)
[90] "Interview with a REAL Vampire Stalker". SeacoastNH.com. Retrieved 2006-06-14.
[91] Bunson, Matthew, *The Vampire Encyclopedia*, Gramercy; 2nd edition (August 1, 2000)

South Asian legend and story may sometimes be rendered as "Vampire" (see the section on "Ancient Beliefs" above). Although vampires have appeared in Japanese cinema since the late 1950s, the folklore behind it is western in origin[92]. However, the Nukekubi is a being whose head and neck detach from its body to fly about seeking human prey at night[93]. There's also the Kitsune who are spiritual vampires that need life force to survive and use magic to obtain it. These creatures acquire this life force from making love with humans.

The Manananggal of Philippine mythology

Legends of female vampire-like beings who can detach parts of their upper body also occur in the Philippines, Malaysia and Indonesia. There are two main vampire-like creatures in the Philippines: the Tagalog Mandurugo ("blood-sucker") and the Visayan Manananggal ("self-segmenter"). The Mandurugo is a variety of the aswang that takes the form of an attractive girl by day, and develops wings and a long, hollow, thread-like tongue by night. The tongue is used to suck up blood from a sleeping victim. The Manananggal is described as

---

[92] Ibid
[93] Hearn, Lafcadio (1903). Kwaidan: Stories and Studies of Strange Things. Boston: Houghton, Mifflin and Company.

being an older, beautiful woman capable of severing its upper torso in order to fly into the night with huge bat-like wings and prey on unsuspecting, sleeping pregnant women in their homes. They use an elongated proboscis-like tongue to suck fetuses from these pregnant women. They also prefer to eat entrails (specifically the heart and the liver) and the phlegm of sick people[94].

The Malaysian Penanggalan may be either a beautiful old or young woman who obtained her beauty through the active use of black magic or other unnatural means, and is most commonly described in local folklore to be dark or demonic in nature. She is able to detach her fanged head which flies around in the night looking for blood, typically from pregnant women[95]. Malaysians would hang jeruju (thistles) around the doors and windows of houses, hoping the Penanggalan would not enter for fear of catching its intestines on the thorns.

The Leyak is a similar being from Balinese folklore[96]. A Kuntilanak or Matianak in Indonesia, or Pontianak or Langsuir in Malaysia, is a woman who died

---

[94] Ramos, Maximo D. (1990) [1971]. *Creatures of Philippine Lower Mythology*. Quezon: Phoenix Publishing.
[95] Bunson, Matthew, *The Vampire Encyclopedia*, Gramercy; 2nd edition (August 1, 2000)
[96] Hoyt, Olga Grunhzit, *Lust for Blood*, Rowman & Littlefield Publishers, Inc., 1990

during childbirth and became undead, seeking revenge and terrorizing villages. She appeared as an attractive woman with long black hair that covered a hole in the back of her neck, with which she sucked the blood of children. Filling the hole with her hair would drive her off. Corpses had their mouths filled with glass beads, eggs under each armpit, and needles in their palms to prevent them from becoming langsuir. This description would also fit the Sundel Bolongs[97].

Jiangshi, sometimes called "Chinese vampires" by Westerners, are reanimated corpses that hop around, killing living creatures to absorb life essence (qì) from their victims. They are said to be created when a person's soul (魄 pò) fails to leave the deceased's body[98].

However, some have disputed the comparison of jiang shi with vampires, as jiang shi are usually mindless creatures with no independent thought. One unusual feature of this monster is its greenish-white furry skin, perhaps derived from fungus or mold growing on corpses[99]. Jiangshi legends have inspired a genre of jiangshi films and literature in Hong Kong and East Asia.

---

[97] Ibid

[98] Suckling, Nigel (2006). *Vampires. London: Facts, Figures & Fun.* p. 31.

[99] de Groot, J.J.M. (1910). "*The Religious System of China*". E.J. Brill.

CHAPTER SEVEN

MODERN BELIEFS

Modern beliefs

In modern fiction, the vampire tends to be depicted as a suave, charismatic villain. Despite the general disbelief in vampiric entities, occasional sightings of vampires are reported. Indeed, vampire hunting societies still exist, although they are largely formed for social reasons. Allegations of vampire attacks swept through the African country of Malawi during late 2002 and early 2003, with mobs stoning one individual to death and attacking at least four others, including Governor Eric Chiwaya, based on the belief that the government was colluding with vampires[100].

In early 1970 local press spread rumors that a vampire haunted High Gate Cemetery in London. Amateur vampire hunters flocked in large numbers to the cemetery.

---

[100] Tenthani, Raphael (23 December 2002). "'Vampires' strike Malawi villages". BBC News. Retrieved 2007-12-29.

Several books have been written about the case, notably by Sean Manchester, a local man who was among the first to suggest the existence of the "High Gate Vampire" and who later claimed to have exorcised and destroyed a whole nest of vampires in the area. In January 2005, rumors circulated that an attacker had bitten a number of people in Birmingham, England, fuelling concerns about a vampire roaming the streets. However, local police stated that no such crime had been reported and that the case appears to be an urban legend.

The female vampire costume

In 2006, a physics professor at the University of Central Florida wrote a paper arguing that it is mathematically impossible for vampires to exist, based on geometric progression. According to the paper, if the first vampire had appeared on 1 January 1600, and it fed once a month (which is less often than what is depicted in films and folklore), and every victim turned into a vampire, then within two and a half years the entire human population of the time would have become vampires[101]. The paper made no attempt to address the credibility of the assumption that every vampire victim would turn into a vampire.

---

[101] *Math vs. vampires: vampires lose, world-science.net*, 25 October 2006.

In one of the more notable cases of vampiric entities in the modern age, the Chupacabra ("goat-sucker") of Puerto Rico and Mexico is said to be a creature that feeds upon the flesh or drinks the blood of domesticated animals, leading some to consider it a kind of vampire. The "Chupacabra hysteria" was frequently associated with deep economic and political crises, particularly during the mid-1990s.

In Europe, where much of the vampire folklore originates, the vampire is usually considered a fictitious being, although many communities may have embraced the revenant for economic purposes. In some cases, especially in small localities, vampire superstition is still rampant and sightings or claims of vampire attacks occur frequently.

In Romania during February 2004, several relatives of Toma Petre feared that he had become a vampire. They dug up his corpse, tore out his heart, burned it, and mixed the ashes with water in order to drink it.

Vampirism and the Vampire lifestyle also represent a relevant part of modern day's occultist movements. The mythos of the vampire, his magical qualities, allure, and predatory archetype express a strong symbolism that can be used in ritual, energy work, and magic, and can even be adopted as a spiritual system. The vampire has been part of

the occult society in Europe for centuries and has spread
into the American sub-culture as well for more than a
decade, being strongly influenced by and mixed with the
neo gothic aesthetics.

CHAPTER EIGHT

OTHER VIEWS OF THE VAMPIRE

In his 1931 treatise *On the Nightmare*, Welsh psychoanalyst Ernest Jones asserted that vampires are symbolic of several unconscious drives and defense mechanisms. Emotions such as love, guilt, and hate fuel the idea of the return of the dead to the grave. Desiring a reunion with loved ones, mourners may project the idea that the recently dead must in return yearn for the same reunion. From this arises the belief that folkloric vampires and revenants visit relatives, particularly their spouses, first.

In cases where there was unconscious guilt associated with the relationship, however, the wish for reunion may be subverted by anxiety. This may lead to repression, which Sigmund Freud had linked with the development of morbid dread. Jones surmised in this case the original wish of a (sexual) reunion may be drastically changed: desire is replaced by fear; love is replaced by sadism, and the object or loved one is replaced by an unknown entity. The sexual aspect may or may not be present. Some modern critics have proposed a simpler theory: People identify with immortal vampires because, by so doing, they overcome, or at least temporarily escape from, their fear of dying.

The innate sexuality of bloodsucking can be seen in its intrinsic connection with cannibalism and folkloric one with incubus-like behavior. Many legends report various beings draining other fluids from victims, an unconscious association with semen being obvious. Finally Jones notes that when more normal aspects of sexuality are repressed, regressed forms may be expressed, in particular sadism; he felt that oral sadism is integral in vampiric behavior.

Political Interpretation

The reinvention of the vampire myth in the modern era is not without political overtones[102]. The aristocratic Count Dracula, alone in his castle apart from a few demented retainers, appearing only at night to feed on his peasantry, is symbolic of the parasitic Ancient regime. In

---

[102] Glover, David (1996). *Vampires, Mummies, and Liberals: Bram Stoker and the Politics of Popular Fiction.* Durham, NC.: Duke University Press.

his entry for "Vampires" in the Dictionnaire Philosophique (1764), Voltaire notices how the end of the 18th century coincided with the decline of the folkloric belief in the existence of vampires but that now "there were stock-jobbers, brokers, and men of business, who sucked the blood of the people in broad daylight; but they were not dead, though corrupted. These true suckers lived not in cemeteries, but in very agreeable palaces". Marx similarly famously defined capital as "dead labor which, vampire-like, lives only by sucking living labor, and lives the more, the more labor it sucks".

In Das Kapital Marx repeatedly refers to capital as a vampire, because of its monstrous metabolism: according to the German philosopher and revolutionary, in fact, capital is capable at once to suck living labor out of the workers and to transform them in an integral part of itself (variable capital)[103]. Werner Herzog, in his Nosferatu the Vampyre, gives this political interpretation an extra ironic twist when protagonist Jonathon Harker, a middle-class solicitor, becomes the next vampire; in this way the capitalist bourgeois becomes the next parasitic class[104].

---

[103] Policante, A. "*Vampires of Capital: Gothic Reflections between horror and hope*" in Cultural Logic, 2010.
[104] Brass, Tom (2000). "*Nymphs, Shepherds, and Vampires: The Agrarian Myth on Film*". Dialectical Anthropology 25 (3/4): 205–237.

Psychopathology

A number of murderers have performed seemingly vampiric rituals upon their victims. Serial killers Peter Kürten and Richard Trenton Chase were both called "vampires" in the tabloids after they were discovered drinking the blood of the people they murdered. Similarly, in 1932, an unsolved murder case in Stockholm, Sweden was nicknamed the "Vampire murder", because of the circumstances of the victim's death[105]. The late-16th-century Hungarian countess and mass murderer Elizabeth Báthory became particularly infamous in later centuries' works, which depicted her bathing in her victims' blood in order to retain beauty or youth[106].

Modern Vampire Subcultures

Vampire lifestyle is a term for a contemporary subculture of people, largely within the Goth subculture, who consume the blood of others as a pastime; drawing from the rich recent history of popular culture related to cult symbolism, horror films, the fiction of Anne Rice, and

---

[105] (Swedish) Linnell, Stig (1993) [1968]. Stockholms spökhus och andra ruskiga ställen. Raben Prisma.
[106] Hoyt, Olga Grunhzit, *Lust for Blood*, Rowman & Littlefield Publishers, Inc., 1990

the styles of Victorian England. Active vampirism within the vampire subculture includes both blood-related vampirism, commonly referred to as sanguine vampirism, and psychic vampirism, or supposed feeding from pranic energy[107].

---

[107] Jon, A. Asbjorn (2002). "*The Psychic Vampire and Vampyre Subculture*". Australian Folklore (12): 143–148.

PART TWO

WEREWOLVES

CHAPTER NINE

WHAT'S A WEREWOLVES

A werewolf, also known as a lycanthrope, is a mythological or folkloric human with the ability to shape shift into a wolf or a therianthropic hybrid wolf-like creature, either purposely or after being placed under a curse or affliction (e.g. via a

Figure 29: Woodcut of a werewolf attack, sent to author

bite or scratch from another werewolf).

The werewolf is a widespread concept in European folklore, existing in many variants which are related by a common development of a Christian interpretation of underlying Indo-European mythology which developed during the medieval period. From the early modern period, werewolf beliefs also spread to the New World with colonialism. Belief in werewolf develops parallel to the belief in witches, in the course of the Late Middle Ages and the Early Modern period.

Figure 30: A man wearing a wolf skin, author's collection

Like the witchcraft trials as a whole, the trial of supposed werewolves emerged in what is now Switzerland (especially the Valais and Vaud) in the early 15th century and spreads throughout Europe in the 16th, peaking in the 17th and subsiding by the 18th century. The persecution of werewolves and the associated folklore is an integral part of the "witch-hunt" phenomenon, albeit a marginal one, accusations of werewolfery being involved in only a small fraction of witchcraft trials[108].

---

[108] Lorey (2000) records 280 known cases; this contrasts with a total number of 12,000 recorded cases of executions for witchcraft, or an estimated grand total of about 60,000, corresponding to 2% or 0.5% respectively. The recorded cases span the period of 1407 to 1725, peaking during the period of 1575–1657.

During the early period, accusations of lycanthropy (transformation into a wolf) were mixed with accusations of wolf-riding or wolf-charming. The case of Peter Stumpp (1589) led to a significant peak in both interest in and persecution of supposed werewolves, primarily in French-speaking and German-speaking Europe. The phenomenon persisted longest in Bavaria and Austria, with persecution of wolf-charmers recorded until well after 1650, the final cases taking place in the early 18th century in Carinthia and Styria[109].

After the end of the witch-trials, the werewolf became of interest in folklore studies and in the emerging Gothic horror genre; werewolf fiction as a genre has pre-modern precedents in medieval romances (e.g. Bisclavret and Guillaume de Palerme) and develops in the 18th century out of the "semi-fictional" chap book tradition. The trappings of horror literature in the 20th century became part of the horror and fantasy genre of modern pop culture.

The word werewolf continues a late Old English wer(e)wulf, a compound of were "adult male human" and wulf "wolf". The only Old High German testimony is in the form of a given name, Weriuuolf, although an early Middle High German werwolf is found in Burchard of Worms and

---

[109] Ibid

Berthold of Regensburg. The word or concept does not occur in medieval German poetry or fiction, gaining popularity only from the 15th century. Middle Latin gerulphus Anglo-Norman garwalf, Old Frankish wariwulf.

Old Norse had the cognate varúlfur, but because of the high importance of werewulves in Norse mythology, there were alternative terms such as ulfhéðinn ("one in wolf-skin", referring still to the totemistic/cultic adoption of wolf-nature rather than the superstitious belief in actual shape-shifting). In modern Scandinavian also kveldulf "evening-wolf", presumably after the name of Kveldulf Bjalfason, a historical berserker of the 9th century who figures in the Icelandic sagas.

The term lycanthropy, referring both to the ability to transform oneself into a wolf and to the act of so doing, comes from Ancient Greek λυκάνθρωπος lukánthropos (from λύκος lúkos "wolf" and ἄνθρωπος, ánthrōpos "human". The word does occur in ancient Greek sources, but only in Late Antiquity, only rarely, and only in the context of clinical lycanthropy described by Galen, where the patient had the ravenous appetite and other qualities of a wolf; the Greek word attains some currency only in Byzantine Greek, featuring in the 10th-century encyclopedia Suda. Use of the Greek-derived lycanthropy in English occurs in learned writing beginning in the later 16th century (first recorded 1584 in <u>Discoverie of Witchcraft</u> by Reginald Scot, who argued against the reality of werewolves; "Lycanthropia is a disease, and not a transformation." v. i. 92), at first explicitly for clinical lycanthropy, i.e. the type of insanity where the patient imagines to have transformed into a wolf, and not in reference to supposedly real shape-shifting. Use of lycanthropy for supposed shape-shifting is much later, introduced ca. 1830.

Greek λυκάνθρωπος and Germanic werewulf are parallel inasmuch as the concept of a shapeshifter becoming a wolf is expressed by means of a compound "wolf-man" or "man-wolf". Latin and the Romance languages do not appear to have a native term for the concept but loaned terms from Greek, Germanic or Slavic; In French loup-garou, the garou is in origin a loan of Frankish wariwulf, recharacterized with the French word for "wolf".

Spanish and Portuguese have the modern loan-translations hombre lobo and lobisomem, respectively (also Galician lobishome). Italian has the Greek licantropo in learned or literary context (as English uses lycanthrope besides the native werewolf), while Italian folklore uses the term lupo mannaro. This latter Italian term however does not necessarily denote a werewolf, but more often concerns stories of enormous and man-eating, but not supernatural, wolves. Romanian loaned the Slavic term as vârcolac.

The werewolf folklore found in Europe harks back to a common development during the Middle Ages, arising in the context of Christianization, and the associated interpretation of pre-Christian mythology in Christian terms. Their underlying common origin can be traced back to Proto-Indo-European mythology, where lycanthropy is reconstructed as an aspect of the initiation of the warrior class. This is reflected in Iron Age Europe in the Tierkrieger depictions from the Germanic sphere, among others. The standard comparative overview of this aspect of Indo-European mythology is McCone (1987). Such transformations of "men into wolves" in pagan cults were associated with the devil from the early medieval perspective.

The concept of the werewolf in Western and Northern Europe is strongly influenced by the role of the wolf in Germanic paganism (e.g. the French loup-garou is ultimately a loan from the Germanic term), but there are related traditions in other parts of Europe which were not necessarily influenced by Germanic tradition, especially in

Slavic Europe and the Balkans, and possibly in areas bordering the Indo-European sphere (the Caucasus) or where Indo-European cultures have been replaced by military conquest in the medieval era (Hungary, Anatolia).[clarification needed]

In his <u>Man into Wolf</u> (1948), Robert Eisler tried to cast the Indo-European tribal names meaning "wolf" or "wolf-men" in terms of "the European transition from fruit gathering to predatory hunting."

Classical Antiquity

A few references to men changing into wolves are found in Ancient Greek literature and mythology. Herodotus, in his Histories, wrote that the Neuri, a tribe he places to the north-east of Scythia, were all transformed into wolves once every year for several days, and then changed back to their human shape. In the second century BC, the Greek geographer Pausanias relates the story of Lycaon, who was transformed into a wolf because he had ritually murdered a child. In accounts by the Bibliotheca (3.8.1) and Ovid (Metamorphoses I.219-239), Lycaon serves human flesh to Zeus, wanting to know if he is really a god. Lycaon's transformation, therefore, is punishment for a crime, considered variously as murder, cannibalism, and impiety. Ovid also relates stories of men who roamed the woods of Arcadia in the form of wolves.

In addition to Ovid, other Roman writers also mentioned lycanthropy. Virgil wrote of human beings transforming into wolves. Pliny the Elder relates two tales of lycanthropy. Quoting Euanthes, he mentions a man who hung his clothes on an ash tree and swam across an Arcadian lake, transforming him into a wolf. On the condition that he attacks no human being for nine years, he would be free to swim back across the lake to resume human form. Pliny also quotes Agriopas regarding a tale of a man who was turned into a wolf after tasting the entrails of a human child, but was restored to human form 10 years later.

In the Latin work of prose, the Satyricon, written about 60 C.E. by Gaius Petronius Arbiter, one of the characters, Niceros, tells a story at a banquet about a friend who turned into a wolf (chs. 61-62). He describes the incident as follows, "*When I look for my buddy I see he'd stripped and piled his clothes by the roadside... He pees in a circle round his clothes and then, just like that, turns into a wolf!... after he turned into a wolf he started howling and then ran off into the woods.*"

In 5th century, even Procopius recorded a werewolf fight in Roman army:

> *And with him eight hundred others perished after shewing themselves brave men in this struggle, and almost all the Isaurians fell with their leaders, without even daring to lift their weapons against the enemy. For they were thoroughly inexperienced in this business, since they had recently left off farming and entered into the perils of warfare, which before that time were unknown to them. And yet just before these very men had been most furious of all for battle because of their ignorance of warfare, and were then reproaching Belisarius with cowardice. They were not in fact all Isaurians but the majority of them were Lycaones (werewolf)*"[110].

---

[110] Procopius, Persian war, Chapter XVIII

CHAPTER TEN

WEREWOLVES IN THE

MEDIEVAL AGES

There was apparently not a widespread belief in werewolves in medieval Europe before the 14th century, though there were no doubt a few examples prior to that time. There were some examples of man-wolf transformations in the Court literature of the time, notably Marie de France's poem Bisclavret (c. 1200), in which the nobleman Bizuneh, for reasons not described in the poem, had to transform into a wolf every week.

When his treacherous wife stole his clothing that he needed to restore him to his human form, he escaped the king's wolf hunt by imploring the king for mercy and accompanied the king thereafter. His behavior at court was so much gentler than when his wife and her new husband appeared at court, that his hateful attack on the couple was deemed justly motivated, and the truth was revealed.

The German word werwolf was first recorded by Burchard von Worms in the 11th Century and then by Bertold of Regensburg in the 13th, but is not found in any medieval German poetry or fiction.

References to werewolves are also rare in early English literature, presumably because whatever significance the "wolf-men" of Germanic paganism had carried, the associated beliefs and practices had been successfully repressed after Christianization.

Figure 31: Ulfhednar

The Germanic pagan traditions associated with wolf-men persisted longest in the Scandinavian Viking Age. King Harald I of Norway is known to have had a body of warriors called Úlfhednar (wolf coated men), which were mentioned in the

Vatnsdœla Saga, Haraldskvæði, and the Völsunga saga, and resemble some werewolf legends.

The Úlfhednar were fighters similar to the berserkers, though they dressed in wolf hides rather than those of bears and were reputed to channel the spirits of these animals to enhance effectiveness in battle[111]. These warriors were resistant to pain and killed viciously in battle, much like wild animals. Úlfhednar and berserkers are closely associated with the Norse god Odin.

Figure 32: Zeus turning a man into a wolf, sent to author

The Scandinavian traditions of this period may have spread to Rus, giving rise to the Slavic "werewolf" tales. The 11th century Belarusian Prince Usiaslau of Polatsk was

---

[111] Woodward, Ian (1979). *The Werewolf Delusion*. Paddington Press.

considered to have been a Werewolf, capable of moving at superhuman speeds, as recounted in The Tale of Igor's Campaign: "*Vseslav the prince judged men; as prince, he ruled towns; but at night he prowled in the guise of a wolf. From Kiev, prowling, he reached, before the cocks' crew, Tmutorokan. The path of Great Sun, as a wolf, prowling, he crossed. For him in Polotsk they rang for matins early at St. Sophia the bells; but he heard the ringing in Kiev.*"

The situation as described during the medieval period gives rise to the dual form of werewolf folklore in Early Modern Europe. On one hand the "Germanic" werewolf, which becomes associated with the witchcraft panic from around 1400 and on the other hand the "Slavic" werewolf or vlkodlak, which becomes associated with the concept of the revenant or "vampire".

The "eastern" werewolf-vampire is found in the folklore of Cebral/Eastern Europe, including Hungary, Romania and the Balkans, while the "western" werewolf-sorcerer is found in France, German-speaking Europe and in the Baltic.

There were numerous reports of werewolf attacks – and consequent court trials – in 16th century France. In some of the cases there was clear evidence against the accused of both murder and cannibalism, but none of being associated with wolves. In other cases people have been terrified by such creatures, such as that of Gilles Garnier in Dole in 1573, where there was clear evidence against what was believed to be a wolf but none against the accused. Over time, the loup-garou eventually ceased to be regarded as a dangerous heretic and reverted to the pre-Christian notion of a "man-wolf-fiend". The lubins or lupins were usually female and shy in contrast to the aggressive loups-garous.

Werewolvery was a common accusation in witch trials throughout history, and it was seen even in the Valais witch trials, one of the earliest such trials which took place in the first half of the 15th century. Likewise, in the Vaud, child-eating werewolves were reported as early as 1448. A peak of attention to lycanthropy came in the late 16th to early 17th century, as part of the European witch-hunts.

A number of treatises on werewolves were written in France during 1595 and 1615 showing that the topic received much attention among the educated class but there were few tales found in the lower classes.

Werewolves were sighted in 1598 in Anjou, and a teenage werewolf was sentenced to life imprisonment in Bordeaux in 1603. Henry Boguet wrote a lengthy chapter about werewolves in 1602. In the Vaud, individuals

believed to be werewolves were convicted in 1602 and in
1624. However, a treatise by a Vaud pastor in 1653,
however, argued that lycanthropy was purely an illusion.
After this, the only further record from the Vaud dates to
1670 and related the tale of a boy who claimed he and his
mother could change themselves into wolves, which was,
however, not taken seriously.

At the beginning of the 17th century witchcraft was
prosecuted by James I of England, who regarded
"warwoolfes" as victims of delusion induced by "a natural
superabundance of melancholic". After 1650, belief in
Lycanthropy had mostly disappeared from French-speaking
Europe, although there were continuing reports of
extraordinary wolf-like beasts (but not werewolves), such
as the Beast of Gévaudan which terrorized the general area
of the former province of Gévaudan, now called Lozère, in
south-central France.

From the years 1764 to 1767, an unknown entity
killed upwards of 80 men, women, and children. The only
part of Europe which showed vigorous interest in
werewolves after 1650 was the Holy Roman Empire. At
least nine works on lycanthropy were printed in Germany
between 1649 and 1679. In the Austrian and Bavarian Alps,
belief in werewolves persisted well into the 18th century.

Until the 20th century, wolf attacks on humans were an occasional, but still widespread feature of life in Europe. Some scholars have suggested that it was inevitable that wolves, being the most feared predators in Europe, were projected into the folklore of evil shapeshifters. This is said to be corroborated by the fact that areas devoid of wolves typically use different kinds of predator to fill the niche; were hyenas in Africa, were tigers in India, as well as were pumas ("runa uturuncu") and were jaguars ("yaguaraté-abá" or "tigre-capiango") in southern South America.

An idea is explored in Sabine Baring-Gould's work _The Book of Werewolves_ is that werewolf legends may have been used to explain serial killings. Perhaps the most famous example is the case of Peter Stumpp (executed in 1589), the German farmer, and alleged serial killer and cannibal, also known as the Werewolf of Bedburg.

CHAPTER ELEVEN

LYCANTHROPY AS A MEDICAL CONDITION

Loath to admit that there might be something unknown to science lurking in the shadows, some modern researchers have tried to explain the reports of werewolf behavior with recognized medical conditions.

Dr Lee Illis of Guy's Hospital in London wrote a paper in 1963 entitled *On Porphyria and the Aetiology of Werewolves*, in which he argues that historical accounts on werewolves could have in fact been referring to victims of congenital porphyria, stating how the symptoms of photosensitivity, reddish teeth and psychosis could have been grounds for accusing a sufferer of being a werewolf[112].

The facts as presented by Illis were argued against by Woodward, who points out how mythological werewolves were almost invariably portrayed as resembling true wolves, and that their human forms were rarely physically conspicuous as porphyria victims[113].

Others have pointed out the possibility that historical werewolves might have been sufferers of hypertrichosis, a hereditary condition manifesting itself in excessive hair growth. After exploring this possibility, Woodward dismissed the idea, as the rarity of the disease ruled it out from happening on a large scale. At the same time, werewolf cases were widespread across medieval Europe[114].

People suffering from Down syndrome have been suggested by some scholars to have been possible originators of werewolf myths[115]. Woodward suggested rabies might be the origin of werewolf beliefs, claiming

---

[112] Illis, L (Jan 1964). "On Porphyria and the Ætiology of Werwolves". Proc R Soc Med 57 (1): 23–6.
[113] Woodward, Ian (1979). *The Werewolf Delusion*. Paddington Press.
[114] Ibid
[115] Lopez, Barry (1978). *Of Wolves and Men*. New York: Scribner Classics.

remarkable similarities between the symptoms of that disease and some of the legends.

Woodward focused on the idea that being bitten by a werewolf could result in the victim turning into one, which suggested the idea of a transmittable disease like rabies[116]. However, the idea that lycanthropy could be transmitted in this way is not part of the original myths and legends and only appears in relatively recent beliefs.

Characteristics of a Werewolf

The beliefs classed together under lycanthropy are far from uniform, and the term is somewhat capriciously applied. The transformation may be temporary or permanent; the were-animal may be the man himself metamorphosed; may be his double whose activity leaves the real man to all appearance unchanged; maybe his soul, which goes forth seeking whom it may devour, leaving its body in a state of trance; or it may be no more than the messenger of the human being, a real animal or a familiar spirit, whose intimate connection with its owner is shown by the fact that any injury to it is believed, by a phenomenon known as repercussion, to cause a corresponding injury to the human being.

---

[116] Woodward, Ian (1979). *The Werewolf Delusion*. Paddington Press.

Werewolves were said in European folklore to bear tell-tale physical traits even in their human form. These included the meeting of both eyebrows at the bridge of the nose, curved fingernails, low-set ears and a swinging stride. One method of identifying a werewolf in its human form was to cut the flesh of the accused, based on the idea that fur would be seen within the wound.

A Russian superstition states that a werewolf can be recognized by bristles under the tongue[117]. The appearance of a werewolf in its animal form varies from culture to culture, though it is most commonly portrayed as being indistinguishable from ordinary wolves save for the fact that it has no tail[118], is often larger, and retains human eyes and voice. According to some Swedish accounts, the werewolf could be distinguished from a regular wolf by the fact that it would run on three legs, stretching the fourth one backwards to look like a tail.

After returning to their human forms, werewolves are usually documented as becoming weak, debilitated and undergoing painful nervous depression[119]. One universally reviled trait in medieval Europe was the werewolf's habit of devouring recently buried corpses, a trait that is

---

[117] Ibid
[118] This is also said to be a characteristic of a witch in animal form.
[119] Woodward, Ian (1979). *The Werewolf Delusion*. Paddington Press.

documented extensively, particularly in the Annales Medico-psychologiques in the 19th century[120]. Fennoscandian werewolves were usually supposed to be old women who possessed poison-coated claws and had the ability to paralyze cattle and children with their gaze.

---

[120] Ibid

CHAPTER TWELVE

HOW TO BECOME A WEREWOLF

Many were sought power over their fellows or suffered from desires that went beyond the ordinary looked for ways to become werewolves. Various methods for becoming a werewolf have been reported, one of the simplest being the removal of clothing and putting on a belt made of wolf skin, probably as a substitute for the assumption of an entire animal skin (which also is frequently described)[121]. In other cases, the body is rubbed with a magic salve[122]. Additionally, it was reported that drinking rainwater out of the footprint of the animal in question or from certain enchanted streams were also

---

[121] Bennett, Aaron. *"So, You Want to be a Werewolf?"* Fate. Vol. 55, no. 6, Issue 627. July 2002.
[122] Ibid

considered effectual modes of accomplishing metamorphosis[123].

The 16th century Swedish writer Olaus Magnus says that the Livonian werewolves were initiated by draining a cup of specially prepared beer and repeating a set formula. Ralston in his _Songs of the Russian People_ gives the form of incantation still familiar in Russia. In Italy, France and Germany, it was said that a man or woman could turn into a werewolf if he or she, on a certain Wednesday or Friday, slept outside on a summer night with the full moon shining directly on his or her face[124].

In other cases, the transformation was supposedly accomplished by satanic allegiance for the most loathsome ends, often for the sake of sating a craving for human flesh. The phenomenon of repercussion, the power of animal metamorphosis, or of sending out a familiar, real or spiritual, as a messenger, and the supernormal powers conferred by association with such a familiar, is also attributed to the magician, male and female, all the world over. There are witch superstitions are closely parallel to, if not identical with, lycanthropic beliefs, the occasional involuntary character of lycanthropy being almost the sole

[123] O'Donnell, Elliot. _Werwolves_. Methuen. London. 1912. pp. 65-67.
[124] Woodward, Ian (1979). _The Werewolf Delusion_. Paddington Press.

distinguishing feature. In another direction the phenomenon of repercussion is asserted to manifest itself in connection with the bush-soul of the West African and the nagual of Central America; but though there is no line of demarcation to be drawn on logical grounds, the assumed power of the magician and the intimate association of the bush-soul or the nagual with a human being are not termed lycanthropy. Nevertheless it will be well to touch on both these beliefs here.

The curse of lycanthropy was also considered by some scholars as being a divine punishment. Werewolf literature shows many examples of God or saints allegedly cursing those who invoked their wrath with werewolfism. Such is the case of Lycaon, who was turned into a wolf by Zeus as punishment for slaughtering one of his own sons and serving his remains to the gods as a dinner. Those who were excommunicated by the Roman Catholic Church were also said to become werewolves[125].

As stated earlier, the power of transforming others into wild beasts was attributed not only to malignant sorcerers, but to Christian saints as well. Omnes angeli, boni et Mali, ex virtute naturali habent potestatem transmutandi corpora nostra ("All angels, good and bad

---

[125] Woodward, Ian (1979). *The Werewolf Delusion*. Paddington Press.

have the power of transmutating our bodies") was the dictum of St. Thomas Aquinas.

St. Patrick was said to have transformed the Welsh king Vereticus into a wolf; Natalis supposedly cursed an illustrious Irish family whose members were each doomed to be a wolf for seven years. In other tales the divine agency is even more direct, while in Russia, again, men supposedly became werewolves when incurring the wrath of the Devil.

A notable exception to the association of Lycanthropy and the Devil comes from a rare and lesser known account of an 80-year-old man named Thiess. In 1692, in Jurgenburg, Livonia, Thiess testified under oath that he and other werewolves were the Hounds of God[126]. He claimed they were warriors who went down into hell to do battle with witches and demons. Their efforts ensured that the Devil and his minions did not carry off the grain from local failed crops down to hell.

Thiess was steadfast in his assertions, claiming that werewolves in Germany and Russia also did battle with the devil's minions in their own versions of hell, and insisted that when werewolves died, their souls were welcomed into

[126] Gershenson, Daniel. *Apollo the Wolf-God.* (Journal of Indo-European Studies, Monograph, 8.) McLean, Virginia: Institute for the Study of Man, 1991

heaven as reward for their service. Thiess was ultimately sentenced to ten lashes for Idolatry and superstitious belief.

Remedies

Various methods have existed for removing the werewolf curse. In antiquity, the Ancient Greeks and Romans believed in the power of exhaustion in curing people of lycanthropy. The victim would be subjected to long periods of physical activity in the hope of being purged of the malady. This practice stemmed from the fact that many alleged werewolves would be left feeling weak and debilitated after committing depredations[127].

In medieval Europe, traditionally, there were said to be three methods one can use to cure a victim of werewolfism;

- medicinally (usually via the use of wolfsbane),
- surgically or by
- exorcism.

However, many of the cures advocated by medieval medical practitioners proved fatal to the patients. A Sicilian belief of Arabic origin holds that a werewolf can be cured of its ailment by striking it on the forehead or scalp with a

---

[127] Woodward, Ian (1979). *The Werewolf Delusion*. Paddington Press.

knife. Another belief from the same culture involves the piercing of the werewolf's hands with nails. Sometimes, less extreme methods were used. In the German lowland of Schleswig-Holstein, a werewolf could be cured if one were to simply address it three times by its Christian name, while one Danish belief holds that simply scolding a werewolf will cure it[128]. Conversion to Christianity is also a common method of removing werewolfism in the medieval period. A devotion to St. Hubert[129] has also been cited as both cure for and protection from lycanthropes.

---

[128] Ibid

[129] Saint Hubertus or Hubert (c. 656–727 A.D.) was the first Bishop of Liège. He was a Christian saint who was the patron saint of hunters, mathematicians, opticians, and metalworkers. Known as the Apostle of the Ardennes, he was called upon to cure rabies until the early 20th century through the use of the traditional St Hubert's Key.

Saint Hubertus was widely venerated during the Middle Ages. The iconography of his legend is entangled with the legend of Saint Eustace. He died 30 May 727 A.D. in Tervuren near Brussels, Belgium. His feast day is November 3.

CHAPTER THIRTEEN

OTHER HAUNTS OF WEREWOLVES

Before the end of the 19th century, the Greeks believed that the corpses of werewolves, if not destroyed, would return to life in the form of wolves or hyenas which prowled battlefields, drinking the blood of dying soldiers. In the same vein, in some rural areas of Germany, Poland and Northern France, it was once believed that people who died in mortal sin came back to life as blood-drinking wolves. These "undead" werewolves would return to their human corpse form at daylight. They were dealt with by decapitation with a spade and exorcism by the parish priest. The head would then be thrown into a stream, where the weight of its sins was thought to weigh it down. Sometimes, the same methods used to dispose of ordinary vampires would be used.

The vampire was also linked to the werewolf in East European countries, particularly Bulgaria, Serbia and Slovenia. In Serbia, the werewolf and vampire are known collectively as vulkodlak[130].

Hungary and Balkans

In Hungarian folklore, werewolves used to live specially in the region of Transdanubia, and it was thought that the ability to change into a wolf was obtained during infancy due to suffering of abuse by the parents or by a curse. At the age of seven the boy or the girl leaves the house and goes hunting by night and can change to person or wolf whenever he wants. The curse can also be obtained when in the adulthood the person passed three times through an arch made of a Birch with the help of a wild rose's spine.

Werewolves were known to exterminate all kind of farm animals, especially sheep. A massive die off of sheep was one way to tell is a werewolf was on the prowl.

The transformation time usually occurred in the Winter solstice, Easter and full moon. Later in the 17th and 18th century, trials in Hungary not only were conducted against witches, but against werewolves too, and many

---

[130] Woodward, Ian (1979). *The Werewolf Delusion*. Paddington Press.

records exist creating connections between both of these creatures of the night. It should also be noted that vampires and werewolves are closely related in Hungary, being both feared in the antiquity.

Among the South Slavs, and also among the Kashubs of what is now northern Poland, there was the belief that if a child was born with hair, a birthmark or a caul on their head, they possessed shape-shifting abilities. Though capable of turning into any animal they wished, it was commonly believed that such people preferred to turn into a wolf[131].

Serbian vulkodlaks traditionally had the habit of congregating annually in the winter months, when they would strip off their wolf skins and hang them from trees. They would then get a hold of another vulkodlaks, skin and burn it, releasing from its curse the vulkodlak from whom the skin came[132].

Caucasus

According to Armenian lore, there are women who, in consequence of deadly sins, are condemned to spend

[131]Willis, Roy; Davidson, Hilda Ellis (1997*). World Mythology: The Illustrated Guide*. Piaktus
[132] Woodward, Ian (1979). *The Werewolf Delusion*. Paddington Press.

seven years in wolf form[133]. In a typical account, a condemned woman is visited by a wolf skin-toting spirit, who orders her to wear the skin, which causes her to acquire frightful cravings for human flesh soon after.

With her better nature overcome, the she-wolf devours each of her own children, then her relatives' children in order of relationship, and finally the children of strangers. She wanders only at night, with doors and locks springing open at her approach. When morning arrives, she reverts to human form and removes her wolf skin. The transformation is generally said to be involuntary, but there are alternate versions involving voluntary metamorphosis, where the women can transform at will.

Americas and Caribbean

The Naskapis believed that the caribou afterlife is guarded by giant wolves which kill careless hunters venturing too near. The Navajo people feared witches in wolf's clothing called "Mai-cob"[134].

---

[133] *The Fables of Mkhitar Gosh* (New York, 1987), translated with an introduction by R. Bedrosian, edited by Elise Antreassian and illustrated by Anahid Janjigian

[134] Lopez, Barry (1978). *Of Wolves and Men*. New York: Scribner Classics

Woodward thought that these beliefs were due to the Norse colonization of the Americas[135]. When the European colonization of the Americas occurred, the pioneers brought their own werewolf folklore with them and were later influenced by the lore of their neighboring colonies and those of the Natives.

Belief in the loup-garou present in Canada, the Upper and Lower Peninsulas of Michigan and upstate New York, originates from French folklore influenced by Native American stories on the Wendigo. In Mexico, there is a belief in a creature called the nahual, which traditionally limits itself to stealing cheese and raping women rather than murdering indiscriminately.

In Haiti, there is a superstition that werewolf spirits known locally as Jé-rouge (red eyes) can possess the bodies of unwitting persons and nightly transform them into cannibalistic lupine creatures. The Haitian jé-rouges typically try to trick mothers into giving away their children voluntarily by waking them at night and asking their permission to take their child, to which the disoriented mother may either reply yes or no. The Haitian jé-rouges differ from traditional European werewolves by their habit

---

[135] Woodward, Ian (1979). *The Werewolf Delusion*. Paddington Press.

of actively trying to spread their lycanthropic condition to others, much like vampires[136].

Werewolves are often depicted as immune to damage caused by ordinary weapons, being vulnerable only to silver objects, such as a silver-tipped cane, bullet or blade; this attribute was first adopted cinematically in *The Wolf Man.*

This negative reaction to silver is sometimes so strong that the mere touch of the metal on a werewolf's skin will cause burns. Current-day werewolf fiction almost exclusively involves lycanthropy being either a hereditary condition or being transmitted like an infectious disease by the bite of another werewolf. In some fiction, the power of the werewolf extends to human form, such as invulnerability to conventional injury due to their healing factor, super-human speed and strength and falling on their feet from high falls. Also aggressiveness and animalistic urges may be intensified and harder to control (hunger, sexual arousal). Usually in these cases the abilities are diminished in human form. In other fiction it can be cured by medicine men or antidotes.

---

[136]Woodward, Ian (1979). *The Werewolf Delusion.* Paddington Press.

Nazi Germany

No discussion of werewolves is complete without a reference to Nazi Germany. Nazi Germany twice used Werwolf (as the mythical creature's name is spelled in German). In 1942-43 it was the codename for one of Hitler's headquarters (Werwolf (Wehrmacht HQ)). In the war's final days it was the name of "Operation Werwolf" aimed at creating a commando force which would operate behind enemy lines as the Allies advanced through Germany itself.

Two fictional depictions of "Operation Werwolf"— the US television series True Blood and the 2012 novel Wolf Hunter, by J.L. Benét—mix the two meanings of "Werwolf" by depicting the 1945 diehard Nazi commandos as being actual werewolves.

PART III

THINGS THAT GO

BUMP IN THE NIGHT

CHAPTER FOURTEEN

ZOMBIES

Figure 33: Recreation of Zombie from author's collection

Though it does not have the long duration of belief that vampires and werewolves have, certainly a major player in the world of the shadows is believed to be the Zombie. The English word "zombie" was first used in the 1838 short story "**The Unknown Painter**", as zombi. The additional "e" was not added until the 1900s[137]. While today, stories of Zombies can be found around the world, it was in mysterious Haiti that the creature was said to first appear.

Haitian tradition

Zombies featured widely in Haitian rural folklore, as dead persons physically revived by the act of necromancy of a bokor sorcerer (the bokor is a witch-like figure to be distinguished from the houngan priests and mambo priestesses of the formal Vodou religion). Zombies remain under the control of the bokor as their personal slaves, since they have no will of their own.

There also exists within the Haitian tradition, an incorporeal type of zombie, the "zombie astral", which is a part of the human soul that is captured by a bokor and used to enhance the bokor's spiritual power. Bokors produce and sell specially-decorated bottles to clients with a zombie astral inside, for the purposes of luck, healing or business success. It is believed that after a time God will take the

---

[137] Gandhi, Lakshmi (15 December 2013). *"Zoinks! Tracing The History Of 'Zombie' From Haiti To The CDC"*. NPR CodeSwitch (in English). NPR. Retrieved 7 March 2014.

soul back and so the zombie is a temporary spiritual entity[138].

It has been suggested that the two types of zombies reflect soul dualism and a belief of Haitian Vodou. Each type of legendary zombie is therefore missing one half of its soul (the flesh or the spirit)[139].

The zombie belief has its roots in traditions brought to Haiti by enslaved Africans, and their subsequent experiences in the New World. It was thought that the Vodou deity Baron Samedi would gather them from their grave to bring them to a heavenly afterlife in Africa ("Guinea"), unless they had offended him in some way, in which case they would be forever a slave after death, as a zombie. A zombie could also be saved by feeding them salt. A number of scholars have pointed out the significance of the zombie figure as a metaphor for the history of slavery in Haiti[140].

While most scholars have associated the Haitian zombie with African cultures, a connection has also been suggested to the island's indigenous Taíno people, partly

---

[138] McAlister, Elizabeth. 1995."*A Sorcerer's Bottle: The Visual Art of Magic in Haiti.*" In Donald J. Cosentino, ed., Sacred Arts of Haitian Vodou. UCLA Fowler Museum of Cultural History, 1995: 304–321
[139] Davis, Wade (1985), *The Serpent and the Rainbow*, New York: Simon & Schuster, pp 186
[140] Wilentz, Amy (2012-10-26). "*A Zombie Is a Slave Forever*". The New York Times. Haiti. Retrieved 31 October 2012.

based on an early account of native shamanist practices written by the Hieronymite monk Ramón Pané, a companion of Christopher Columbus[141].

The Haitian zombie phenomenon first attracted widespread international attention during the United States occupation of Haiti (1915 - 1934), when a number of case histories of purported "zombies" began to emerge. The first popular book covering the topics was William Seabrook's **The Magic Island** (1929).

Seabrooke cited the Haitian criminal code as what he considered official recognition of zombies - Article 246 (passed 1864), later to be used in promotional materials for the 1932 film White Zombie, reads in part:

> "*Also shall be qualified as attempted murder the employment which may be made by any person of substances which, without causing actual death, produce a lethargic coma more or less prolonged. If, after the administering of such substances, the person has been buried, the act shall be considered murder no matter what result follows.*"[

In 1937, while researching folklore in Haiti, Zora Neale Hurston encountered the case of a woman who

---

[141] Whitehead, Neal L. (2011). *Of Cannibals and Kings*: Primal Anthropology in the Americas. Penn State Press. pp. 39 – 41.

appeared in a village, and a family claimed she was Felicia Felix-Mentor, a relative who had died and been buried in 1907 at the age of 29. However, the woman had been examined by a doctor, who found on X-ray that she did not have the leg fracture that Felix-Mentor was known to have had[142]. Hurston pursued rumors that the affected persons were given a powerful psychoactive drug, but she was unable to locate individuals willing to offer much information. She wrote: "*What is more, if science ever gets to the bottom of Vodou in Haiti and Africa, it will be found that some important medical secrets, still unknown to medical science, give it its power, rather than gestures of ceremony.*[143]"

Chemical Hypothesis

Several decades after Hurston's work, Wade Davis, a Harvard ethno botanist, presented a pharmacological case for zombies in a 1983 paper in the Journal of Ethnopharmacology[144], and later in two popular books, The

---

[142] Mars, Louis P. (1945). "*Media life zombies*". Man 45 (22): 38–40
[143] Hurston, Zora Neale. *Dust Tracks on a Road.* 2nd Ed. (1942: Urbana: University of Illinois Press, 1984, p. 205).
[144] Davis, Wade (1983), *The Ethnobiology of the Haitian Zombie*, Journal of Ethnopharmacology, 9: 85-104.

Serpent and the Rainbow[145] (1985) and *Passage of Darkness: The Ethnobiology of the Haitian Zombie*[146] (1988).

Davis traveled to Haiti in 1982 and, as a result of his investigations, claimed that a living person can be turned into a zombie by two special powders being introduced into the blood stream (usually via a wound). The first, coup de poudre (French: "powder strike"), includes tetrodotoxin (TTX), a powerful and frequently fatal neurotoxin found in the flesh of the puffer fish (order Tetraodontidae).

The second powder consists of dissociative drugs such as datura. Together, these powders were said to induce a deathlike state in which the will of the victim would be entirely subjected to that of the bokor. Davis also popularized the story of Clairvius Narcisse, who was claimed to have succumbed to this practice. The most ethically questioned and least scientifically explored ingredient of the powders is part of a recently buried child's brain[147].

---

[145] Davis, Wade (1985), *The Serpent and the Rainbow*, New York: Simon & Schuster, pp 186
[146] Davis, Wade, *Passage of Darkness: The Ethnobiology of the Haitian Zombie*, University of North Carolina Press, 1988
[147] Ibid

The process described by Davis was an initial state of deathlike suspended animation, followed by re-awakening — typically after being buried — into a psychotic state. The psychosis induced by the drug and psychological trauma was hypothesized by Davis to reinforce culturally learned beliefs and to cause the individual to reconstruct their identity as that of a zombie, since they "knew" they were dead, and had no other role to play in the Haitian society. Societal reinforcement of the belief was hypothesized by Davis to confirm for the zombie individual the zombie state, and such individuals were known to hang around in graveyards, exhibiting attitudes of low affect.

Davis's claim has been criticized, particularly the suggestion that Haitian witch doctors can keep "zombies" in a state of pharmacologically induced trance for many years[148]. In support of his theory, he point to symptoms of TTX poisoning which range from numbness and nausea to paralysis — particularly of the muscles of the diaphragm — unconsciousness, and death, but do not include a stiffened gait or a deathlike trance. According to psychologist Terence Hines, the scientific community dismisses tetrodotoxin as the cause of this state, and Davis'

---

[148] Booth, W. (1988), "*Voodoo Science*", Science, 240: 274–277.

assessment of the nature of the reports of Haitian zombies is viewed as overly credulous[149].

Social Hypothesis

If the voodoo solution and the use of drugs do not explain Zombies then there is what is referred to as the social cause. Scottish psychiatrist R. D. Laing highlighted the link between social and cultural expectations and compulsion, in the context of schizophrenia and other mental illness, suggesting that schizogenesis may account for some of the psychological aspects of zombification[150]. Particularly, this suggests cases where schizophrenia manifests a state of catatonia.

Roland Littlewood, professor of anthropology and psychiatry, published a study supporting a social explanation of the zombie phenomenon in the medical journal **The Lancet** in 1997[151].

The social explanation sees observed cases of people identified as zombies as a culture-bound syndrome, with a particular cultural form of adoption practiced in

---

[149] Hines, Terence; "*Zombies and Tetrodotoxin*"; Skeptical Inquirer; May/June 2008; Volume 32, Issue 3; Pages 60–62.
[150] Oswald, Hans Peter (2009). *Vodoo. BoD* – Books on Demand. p. 39
[151] Littlewood, Roland; Chavannes Douyon (11 October 1997). "*Clinical findings in three cases of zombification*". The Lancet 350 (9084): 1094 – 1096

Haiti that unites the homeless and mentally ill with grieving families who see them as their "returned" lost loved ones, as Littlewood summarizes his findings in an article in **Times Higher Education**:

> *"I came to the conclusion that although it is unlikely that there is a single explanation for all cases where zombies are recognized by locals in Haiti, the mistaken identification of a wandering mentally ill stranger by bereaved relatives is the most likely explanation in many cases. People with a chronic schizophrenic illness, brain damage or learning disability are not uncommon in rural Haiti, and they would be particularly likely to be identified as zombies."*

African and Related Legends

A Central or West African origin for the Haitian zombie has been postulated based on two etymologies in the Kongo language, nzambi ("god") and zumbi ("fetish"). This root helps form the names of several deities, including the Kongo creator deity Nzambi a Mpungu and the Louisiana serpent deity Li Grand Zombi (a local version of the Haitian Damballa), but it is in fact a generic word for a divine spirit[152]. The common African conception of beings under these names is more similar to the incorporeal "zombie astral"[153], as in the Kongo Nkisi spirits.

A related, but also often incorporeal, undead being is the jumbee of the English-speaking Caribbean, considered to be of the same etymology[154]; in the French West Indies also, local "zombies" are recognized, but these are of a more general spirit nature[155].

The idea of physical zombie-like creatures is present in some South African cultures, where they are called xidachane in Sotho/Tsonga and maduxwane in Venda. In some communities it is believed that a dead person can be zombified by a small child[156]. It is said that the spell can be broken by a powerful enough sangoma.

It is also believed in some areas of South Africa that witches can zombify a person by killing and possessing the

---

[152] Moreman, Christopher M.; Rushton, Cory James (2011). *Race, Oppression and the Zombie: Essays on Cross-Cultural Appropriations of the Caribbean Tradiion,*. McFarland. p. 3.
[153] McAlister, Elizabeth. 1995."*A Sorcerer's Bottle: The Visual Art of Magic in Haiti.*" In Donald J. Cosentino, ed., Sacred Arts of Haitian Vodou. UCLA Fowler Museum of Cultural History, 1995: 304–321
[154] Moore, Brian L. (1995). *Cultural Power, Resistance, and Pluralism: Colonial Guyana, 1838-1900.* University of California Press. pp. 147 – 149.
[155] Dayan, Joan (1998). *Haiti, History, and the Gods.* University of California Press. p. 37.
[156] Marinovich, Greg; Silva Joao (2000). *The Bang-Bang Club Snapshots from a Hidden War.* William Heinemann. p. 84.

victim's body in order to force it into slave labor. After rail lines were built to transport migrant workers, stories emerged about "witch trains". These trains appeared ordinary, but were staffed by zombified workers controlled by a witch. The trains would abduct a person boarding at night and the person would then either be turned into a zombified worker, or beaten and thrown from the train a distance away from the original location[157].

---

[157] Niehaus, Isak (June 2005). "*Witches and Zombies of the South African Lowveld: Discourse, Accusations and Subjective Reality*". The Journal of the Royal Anthropological Institute 11 (2): 197–198.

CHAPTER FIFTEEN

SHADOW PEOPLE

A shadow person (also known as a shadow figure, shadow being or black mass) is an alleged paranormal entity. Though many have reported seeing them, it is believed by skeptics to be a type of hallucination where the subject perceives a patch of shadow in their peripheral vision to be a living, humanoid figure. However, paranormal researcher Heidi Hollis has expressed the belief that shadow people are malevolent supernatural entities[158].

History of Shadow People

A number of religions, legends, and belief systems describe shadowy spiritual beings or supernatural entities such as shades of the underworld, and various shadowy

[158] Ahlquist, Diane (2007). *The Complete Idiot's Guide to Life After Death*. USA: Penguin Group. p. 122

creatures have long been a staple of folklore and ghost stories.

Several physiological and psychological conditions can account for reported experiences of shadow people. These include sleep paralysis, illusions, or hallucinations brought on by physiological or psychological circumstances, drug use or side effects of medication, and the interaction of external agents on the human body. Another reason that could be behind the illusion is sleep deprivation, which may lead to hallucinations.

Modern folklore

Heidi Hollis' appearances on the Coast to Coast AM late night radio talk show helped popularize modern beliefs in shadow people. Hollis described them as dark silhouettes with human shapes and profiles that flicker in and out of peripheral vision, and claimed that people had reported the figures attempting to "jump on their chest and choke them". She, like many others, believes they can be repelled by invoking "the name of Jesus".

Although participants in online discussion forums devoted to paranormal and supernatural topics describe shadow people as menacing, other believers and paranormal authors do not agree that shadow people are either evil, helpful, or neutral, and some even speculate that shadow people may be the extra-dimensional inhabitants of another universe. Some paranormal investigators and authors such as Chad Stambaugh claim to have recorded images of shadow people on video.

In Popular Culture

While many profess to never have heard of these creatures, they have appeared in many works, both written and on film.

Shadow people, described as "Shadow Men", feature prominently in the 2007 novel John Dies at the End.

The 2013 movie Shadow People depicts a sleep study conducted during the 1970s in which patients report seeing shadowy intruders before dying in their sleep. The movie follows a radio host and CDC investigator who research the story, and the story is claimed to be "based on true events".

The popular fantasy book series A Song of Ice and Fire, and its TV adaptation Game of Thrones, features a magical ability called "shadow binding", in which some part of the essence of a man's soul is trapped in a woman's womb through a sexual ritual. This essence coalesces into a "shadow baby" or "shadow demon" which is then birthed.

It possesses magical abilities which allow it to slide through tight spaces, travel at high speed, and cut through solid steel.

"This scares me and I don't know what it is. I have been seeing them since I was a little girl. Always outta the corner of my eye a tall black shadow. I always feel like something or someone is by me. Last night I went down to my bedroom. There it was. Standing next to my dresser. I ran upstairs crying to my mom. She went down and looked saying it was only 'cause I was overtired. But I KNOW what I saw. It was so scary. I don't know what it is. I need all the help I can get!" – Jessica's cry for help, 10, January 2010.

Tales of walking Shadows come from across the world. Some of these Shadow People wander through the periphery of our lives; others stay for years. People can rarely make out features of these darker-than-night, human shaped entities other than an occasional set of blazing red eyes. Shadow People often appear dressed as a Medieval monk, wearing a fedora, or bald and sexless. These entities may simply trek through our bedroom at night never to be seen again, while others may lurk in doorways, just watching, day after day. Still others attack with energy-draining fear.

What Are They?

I've studied the Shadow People phenomena for over twenty years, and have come to the conclusion the term "Shadow People" is actually a catchall for entities that exhibit certain characteristics – but their origins can be wildly different. Through research and personal experience, I've categorized these creatures by behavior.

- *Benign Shadows*: Shadow People that seem to travel briefly through a person's life. I saw these entities as a child. They appeared to walk with purpose through my room, never acknowledging me, and never straying from their path. I never felt an unholy fear, just the fear of watching a dark human-shaped trespasser walk past my bed.

- *Negative Shadows*: Although these Shadow People tend to simply lurk, they are associated with a feeling of unnatural terror.

- *Red-Eyed Shadows*: These entities are always negative, but stare at experiencers with blazing red eyes. Victims often say they feel this creature feed from their fear.

- *Hooded Shadows*: Dressed as an ancient monk, people who encounter these Shadow People feel a deep rage bubbling behind the black cowl.

- *The Hat Man*: This entity is the most curious. Dressed in a fedora, and sometimes appearing to wear an old-time business suit, the Hat Man appears to people in cultures across the planet.

Shadow People may be demonic entities, ghosts, inter-dimensional travelers, or other denizens of the dark realm we call the Unknown. Regardless of their label, Shadow People could very well be more than just one type of being. Brad Steiger, author of "Shadow World," has studied the paranormal for more than 50 years and agrees that there are many possible explanations for Shadow People. *"I would say that experiencers are seeing all of the above and giving them/it the name of Shadow People."*

Whatever these entities are, they're shocking to those who see them.

A gray sheet of clouds stretched across the sky as 12-year-old Doug ran to the corner store. *"It was overcast but not raining, and in the middle of the afternoon,"* Doug said. The day was shadowless, and decades later he still doesn't know what he saw on his way home from the store, arms laden with food. At first, he thought it was a friend.

"As I approached the corner to turn onto my street, I saw something black sticking beyond the bushes in the front of my house," Doug said. *"I yelled, 'Andre,' and started running toward my driveway where the bushes are."*

The dark figure wasn't his friend Andre. A black, man-shaped Shadow grew from behind the bushes in this quiet afternoon and began running toward Doug's house. *"After a few steps I saw the Shadow running down my driveway toward the back yard,"* he said. *"I ran up the driveway to the gate that leads to my back yard. I couldn't believe my eyes."*

Doug stood at the gate as the black Shadow in the shape of a man ran across his yard and disappeared through a fence. *"I was shocked,"* he said. *"I couldn't stop thinking about it. This thing; what could it be? Why was it black when most stereotypical stories said that ghosts were white? Could this be demonic? Could it be like me, just a person?"*

What did Doug see? Was it a ghost or a demon? Maybe it was a dimensional traveler? Or was it all in his mind?

Science

"I've been visited by what I presume to be the same Shadow three times in my life, and the memories have haunted me ever since. When I was six, I saw it at my dad's new house, towering over my bed. I couldn't move, and I don't remember what happened next. All I remember is trying to scream, but there was this horrible weight on my chest." – Luke Purdy

Most of the Shadow People encounters that have been collected over the years are readily explainable. The experiencer wakes to find a black, human figure standing in the doorway of their bedroom, or leaning over their bed, just watching. A tightness grips their chest like the weight of a person is upon them. They can't breathe. Suddenly the choking eases and the Shadow being is gone. This type of encounter is common, and psychology has a name for it – sleep paralysis.

April Haberyan, a psychology professor at Northwest Missouri State University, said most Shadow People encounters are probably the product of dreams. When people sleep and enter the REM phase, "it's very common for them to see things," Haberyan said. The fear, the paralysis, and the entities are normal. "There are hormones in REM sleep that paralyze the major muscle groups and it's called paradoxical sleep," she said. "(Although) this happens during REM, these people don't stay asleep and the hormones are still in their bodies. It can last up to eight minutes and they feel pressure on their chest and can see people." When the experiencer becomes fully awake, the Shadow Person encounter is over – all that's left is the fear.

Other Shadow People encounters – as well as those of ghosts/UFOs/Bigfoot for that matter – can be attributed to the same trick of light and shadow that allows us to see faces in clouds and carpets. These sightings can also be from electrical stimulation to certain parts of the brain, or drugs. Chemist Rick Toomey said anything that throws off the chemical balance of the brain causes all sorts of problems. "All sensation is in the nervous system and its all chemistry," he said. "If every neurotransmitter is chemistry, you can wreak havoc with that."

However, many encounter Shadow People in full consciousness and full daylight, removing the logical, scientific answers, and leaving something terrible.

The Religious World

"My best friend, when he was a boy he was laying on his bed with the lights on. A shadowy figure emerged

from his closet and moved towards his bedside. The Shadow being reached out a finger and touched my buddy's leg. He screamed and the figure vanished, and his folks were there in moments. My friend's father noticed that the closet door was open, and his parents knew he NEVER slept without it closed. The black spot on his leg remained visible for several years, but the Shadow being never returned. To this day my friend has no idea what happened, but he does know one thing – it was real." – Paul Sycros

Although most reported Shadow People encounters involve an entity simply appearing and disappearing, many aren't that innocent. Negative Shadows, Red-Eyed Shadows, and Hooded Shadows, all bring a feeling of horror when they step into someone's life. These creatures are known by different names, demons, jinn, dark shadows, sgili, but their nature is the same.

Bishop James Long, pastor of St. Christopher Old Catholic Church in Louisville, Kentucky, has studied demonology for years and knows Shadow People well – to him they are something evil. "Shadow People must be taken seriously and they can be quite dangerous," he said. "When a human spirit tries to manifest itself, its form is black or otherwise known as Shadow. It is energy trying to manifest itself so that it can appear to have the physical characteristics it had when living on earth." These entities can move, communicate, and attack, drawing energy from their human victim. "Certainly Shadows that attack are demonic in nature and should be avoided at all times," Long said. "I would strongly encourage anyone who witnesses a dark Shadow to be careful."

Cody Lilly's family has encountered this type of Shadow for years, a black, human-shaped figure, featureless except for a wide-brimmed hat. "We called him the Cowboy because he kind of looked like the Marlboro man," Lilly said. The Cowboy stepped into Lilly's life his sophomore year of high school in Clarinda, Iowa, and visited almost nightly for two years, pacing about his room, waiting for something. The entity, with fiery red eyes, never spoke, and never approached him, but Lilly knew why it was there – it hungered. "It was feeding," Lilly said, convinced the Cowboy was absorbing energy from his terror. "The first time I saw it I was completely incapacitated by how scared I was of it."

Lilly soon went to college thirty miles south and the visits stopped until after graduation in 2011 when he moved to Nebraska. "My girlfriend that is now my fiancée is in Kansas City and I'm in Omaha. I was crashing with friends here," he said. "My car started acting up; I'm in the process of looking for a job, finding an apartment, buying an engagement ring. I had a lot of stuff on my plate, which might have brought on what happened." What happened was the Cowboy. "I'm sitting in my car on the phone with my mom. I don't know much about cars, but my mom does."

As Lilly described the car's behavior to his mother, he noticed a movement in the corner of his right eye. Lilly turned toward the passenger side window and saw it – the Shadow Man that once tormented him in the night. The Cowboy. "It was full on. A Shadow Person in an old fedora," Lilly said. "It was standing there. It leaned over like it's bending to look at me."

As Lilly stared in horror at this red-eyed Shadow Man in full daylight, the Cowboy reached out its arm and knocked on the car window. "It knocked two times," Lilly said. "After it knocked it dissolved in my vision. It just showed up, knocked on my window and was gone." Lilly wonders if the Cowboy wanted to let him know it was still around. "It's been quite some time that I saw him," he said. "I'm just kind of thinking he just showed up. I was feeling stressed out and I think he showed up just to feed on that."

In Islam, the supernatural Jinn can be a companion, or a dark, Shadowy predator. "Jinns are invisible entities believed in by most all Muslims and Middle Eastern folklore," said religion expert, Dashti Namaste. "Jinns get in and out of human spheres regularly, and it is believed that any human is able to make contact with a Jinn." Although Jinn can be benevolent, some Jinn are wicked, appearing as dark figures that lurk in ruins and cemeteries, waiting for an unsuspecting human soul to stumble by. The wicked Jinn, much like the demons of Christianity, are deceivers and may present themselves as the ghost of a loved one to insert themselves into a human's life.

Wahde, a Cherokee, said the nature of Shadow beings in the American Indian tradition are just as dark. "They're humanoid shaped, but not proportionate to a normal person," Wahde said. "Their appearance is more monstrous in nature." These Shadow beings are the product of medicine men that have strayed from the path of healing. "There seem to be a classification of spiritual beings that are Shadow for the most part. These things can be manipulated by bad medicine or bad magic," Wahde said. "They either take that form to attack other people, or they use some other spiritual being as a spiritual attack." In the Cherokee language, these dark medicine people are sgili, or witch. "They're still alive to some degree, but they're not necessarily considered human."

Ghosts

"*I have a young boy shadow/spirit in my home. He appears as a solid black cutout-like figure. He is a prankster, too, but he's NOT mean, or evil. He lets us know he's here at times by playing with the animals. Kittens, dogs, puppies, etc. PLAY, not mean. The dogs and puppies are wagging their tails. He moves my Barbies if he really wants my attention. And the other day he didn't want the door to his room closed, so he opened it. He's a good kid.*"
– Kim Tamsor

A family sees a black figure come down the stairs at the same time at night, turn into the kitchen and disappear. A dark man in an out-of-date suit walks through a child's bedroom and down the hallway. Some Shadow People encounters – benign ones like these – could very well be disembodied spirits wandering the earth. D.H. Parsons, president of The Bliss-Parsons Institute of Metaphysics in Columbia, Missouri, has encountered many Shadow People while investigating a haunting. Although many fellow investigators consider Shadow People demonic, Parsons doesn't necessarily agree. "*My feeling is that a Shadow*

Person is another representation of a residual memory of a person who had such a strong personality in life, that a bit of their energy remained here in this dimension after their spirit crossed over," Parsons said. *"Most of the time the spirit beings are either friendly to us, or confused by us, or curious as to why we are there. But they have never done us any harm, not even the Shadows."*

Not so for eighteen-year-old Dave Stanfield. Stanfield didn't expect something to be waiting for him in his room when he woke. Something was – something dark. A strange feeling pulled Stanfield from a deep sleep. As he lay in the gray room, staring at his bedroom wall, he saw it. "I woke for no reason, had no weird dreams, and I wasn't groggy or half asleep," he said. "My room was dark other than some stray beams coming through the blinds, and I could see a man, darker than the night like a void."

The figure stood at the end of the bed. "I could only make out the silhouette of his head and shoulders. The rest of him just went straight to the floor," Stanfield said. "There were no legs or feet. No red eyes, no facial features whatsoever." Terrified, Stanfield slid low in bed, pulling the covers slowly over his face, watching the black, man-shaped figure standing over him until his blankets hid the horror from his view and Stanfield fell back to sleep.

Stanfield is now 29, and although he doesn't know what this Shadow Being was, he knows he saw it – and it haunts him still. "Only in the past couple of years have I been able to find anything on the subject matter," Stanfield said. "It's almost like re-victimization when reading stories from other people that describe experiences like mine. I never knew it could be so widespread and am still dealing with the shock."

But, as with Parsons' encounters, this being didn't harm Stanfield. At least not physically.

Interdimensional travelers

Most Shadow People encounters are benign, a dark figure lingering in the corners of your life, watching. Could these entities simply be watching us from a realm barely removed from our own? Marie Jones, author of books exploring science and the paranormal, thinks other dimensions could be homes of Shadow People. "In my research into quantum and theoretical physics, I came across ... concepts that really opened up the possibilities to me that entities from somewhere else could be coming here" Jones said.

One of these concepts is wrapped around different dimensions. "Theoretically, if these infinite other universes exist, we really should not physically be able to access them," Jones said. "Yet even theoretical physicists entertain the thought that perhaps the laws of physics on the other side allow for some crossover."

Clark Kent's grandfather died in 1977 and his grandmother moved to a small apartment leaving her old house empty. Shortly after, ten-year-old Kent's family moved in. *"My first friend in the new neighborhood was my next-door neighbor, Jim,"* Kent said. *"We are good friends to this day."* On a day in 1979, Kent invited Jim to his house to play Ping Pong – and it's haunted him since.

That day after school, Kent and Jim had about two hours before Kent's parents came home from work, which meant Ping Pong in the basement between peeks at the forbidden stash of Playboys in a dusty alcove. It was there Kent saw something he didn't expect. *"During our game, I was facing the alcove,"* Kent said. *"At a certain point, something caught my attention."* Standing in the alcove was the shadow of a man wearing a fedora.

"It was creepy, and I had to pause," Kent said. *"I could not figure out how any combination of the boxes could cast such a shadow. Then it moved."*

Kent stood at the Ping Pong table, staring at dark figure watching him from the alcove. He then quickly looked at Jim who was looking at him. *"He realized I had seen something,"* Kent said. *"I was struck by the realization that no man was casting a shadow on the wall, the Shadow was solid and was not attached to any object. I turned and scrambled up the stairs with Jim right behind me."* At the top of the stairs, their breath coming fast and heavy, Kent slammed and latched the basement door, then "looked at Jim with wide eyes."

Jim denied seeing the Shadow man that day and for nearly thirty years after. As the two met for a long needed reunion, Kent mentioned the Shadow Man in his basement. *"Jim sunk into his chair and spoke in a whisper, 'I'll never forget that hat.' I was stunned,"* Kent said. Then he asked the same question he'd asked three decades ago, did you see it? *"Yes, I did,"* Jim told him. *"I was scared."*

But did this entity, this watcher, step into Kent's life from a parallel universe?

Although some physicists entertain the idea of these multiple universes, physicist David Richardson isn't eager to join them. *"I hate to bring this up in this context, but if there were extra dimensions ... (Shadow People) might actually be people,*" he said. "*I'm skeptical of that, but it's possible. We're just starting to figure out that sort of stuff.*"

Ghost? Demon? Jinn? Sgili? Traveler? Regardless of the nature of these entities, regardless of their intentions, the advice for each encounter is the same – proceed with caution.

CHAPTER SIXTEEN

BIG FOOT

Bigfoot, also known as Sasquatch, is the name given to a cryptid ape- or hominid-like creature that some people believe inhabits forests, mainly in the Pacific Northwest region of North America. Bigfoot is usually described as a large, hairy, bipedal humanoid. The term Sasquatch is an anglicized derivative of the Halkomelem word sásq'ets.

Most scientists discount the existence of Bigfoot and consider it to be a combination of folklore, misidentification, and hoax, rather than a living animal, because of the lack of physical evidence and the large numbers of creatures that would be necessary to maintain a breeding population. Scientists Grover Krantz and Jeffrey Meldrum have focused research on the creature for the greater parts of their careers.

Description

Bigfoot is described in reports as a large hairy ape-like creature, in a range of 2–3 m (6.6-9.8 ft) tall, weighing in excess of 500 pounds (230 kg), and covered in dark brown or dark reddish hair. Purported witnesses have described large eyes, a pronounced brow ridge, and a large, low-set forehead; the top of the head has been described as rounded and crested, similar to the sagittal crest of the male gorilla. Bigfoot is commonly reported to have a strong, unpleasant smell by those who claim to have encountered it. The enormous footprints for which it is named have been as large as 24 inches (60 cm) long and 8 inches (20 cm) wide. While most casts have five toes — like all known apes — some casts of alleged Bigfoot tracks have had numbers ranging from two to six. Some have also contained claw marks, making it likely that a portion came from known animals such as bears, which have five toes and claws. Proponents claim that Bigfoot is omnivorous and mainly nocturnal.

History

Before 1958

Wildmen stories are found among the indigenous population of the Pacific Northwest. The legends existed before a single name for the creature. They differed in their details both regionally and between families in the same community. Similar stories of wildmen are found on every continent except Antarctica. Ecologist Robert Michael Pyle argues that most cultures have human-like giants in their folk history: "We have this need for some larger-than-life creature."

Members of the Lummi tell tales about Ts'emekwes, the local version of Bigfoot. The stories are similar to each other in the general descriptions of Ts'emekwes, but details about the creature's diet and activities differed between family stories.

Some regional versions contained more nefarious creatures. The stiyaha or kwi-kwiyai were a nocturnal race that children were told not to say the names of lest the monsters hear and come to carry off a person—sometimes to be killed. In 1847, Paul Kane reported stories by the native people about skoocooms: a race of cannibalistic wildmen living on the peak of Mount St. Helens. The skoocooms appear to have been regarded as supernatural, rather than natural.

Less menacing versions such as the one recorded by Reverend Elkanah Walker exist. In 1840, Walker, a Protestant missionary, recorded stories of giants among the

Native Americans living in Spokane, Washington. The Indians claimed that these giants lived on and around the peaks of nearby mountains and stole salmon from the fishermen's nets.

Local legends were compiled by J. W. Burns in a series of Canadian newspaper articles in the 1920s. Each language had its own name for the local version. Many names meant something along the lines of "wild man" or "hairy man" although other names described common actions it was said to perform (e.g., eating clams). Burns coined the term Sasquatch, which is from the Halkomelem sásq'ets and used it in his articles to describe a hypothetical single type of creature reflected in the stories. Burns' articles popularized the legend and its new name, making it well known in western Canada before it gained popularity in the United States.

After 1958

In 1951, Eric Shipton photographed what he described as a Yeti footprint, which generated considerable attention and led to the story of the Yeti entering popular consciousness. The notoriety of ape-men grew over the decade, culminating in 1958 when large footprints were found in Del Norte County, California by bulldozer operator Gerald Crew. Sets of large tracks appeared multiple times around a road-construction site in Bluff Creek. After not being taken seriously about what he was seeing, Crew brought in his friend, Bob Titmus, to cast the prints in plaster. The story was published in the Humboldt Times along with a photo of Crew holding one of the casts.

Locals had been calling the unseen track-maker "Big Foot" since the late summer, which Humboldt Times columnist Andrew Genzoli shortened to "Bigfoot" in his article. Bigfoot gained international attention when the story was picked up by the Associated Press. Following the death of Ray Wallace – a local logger – his family attributed the creation of the footprints to him. The wife of L.W. "Scoop" Beal, the editor of the Humboldt Standard, which later combined with the Humboldt Times, in which Genzoli's story had appeared, has stated that her husband was in on the hoax with Wallace.

1958 was a watershed year not just for the Bigfoot story itself but also for the culture that surrounds it. The first Bigfoot hunters appeared following the discovery of footprints at Bluff Creek, California. Within a year, Tom Slick, who had funded searches for Yeti in the Himalayas earlier in the decade, organized searches for Bigfoot in the area around Bluff Creek.

As Bigfoot has become better known and a phenomenon in popular culture, sightings have spread throughout North America. In addition to the Pacific Northwest, the Great Lakes region and the Southeastern United States have had many reports of Bigfoot sightings. The debate over the legitimacy of Bigfoot sightings reached a peak in the 1970s, and Bigfoot has been regarded as the first widely popularized example of pseudoscience in American culture.

Prominent Reported Sighting

About a third of all reports of Bigfoot sightings are concentrated in the Pacific Northwest, with most of the remaining reports spread throughout the rest of North America. Some Bigfoot advocates, such as John Willison Green, have postulated that Bigfoot is a worldwide phenomenon. The most notable reports include:

- 1924: Prospector Albert Ostman claimed to have been abducted by Sasquatch and held captive by the creatures in British Columbia.
- 1924: Fred Beck claimed that he and four other miners were attacked one night in July 1924, by several "ape-men" throwing rocks at their cabin in an area later called Ape Canyon, Washington. Beck

said the miners shot and possibly killed at least one of the creatures, precipitating an attack on their cabin, during which the creatures bombarded the cabin with rocks and tried to break in. The supposed incident was widely reported at the time. Beck wrote a book about the alleged event in 1967, in which he argued that the creatures were mystical beings from another dimension, claiming that he had experienced psychic premonitions and visions his entire life of which the ape-men were only one component. Speleologist William Halliday argued in 1983 that the story arose from an incident in which hikers from a nearby camp had thrown rocks into the canyon. There are also local rumors that pranksters harassed the men and planted faked footprints.

- 1941: Jeannie Chapman and her children said they had escaped their home when a 7.5 foot (2.3 m) tall Sasquatch approached their residence in Ruby Creek, British Columbia.

- 1958: Bulldozer operator Jerry Crew took to a newspaper office a cast of one of the enormous footprints he and other workers had seen at an isolated work site at Bluff Creek, California. The crew was overseen by Wilbur L. Wallace, brother of Raymond L. Wallace. After Ray Wallace's death, his children came forward with a pair of 16-inch (41 cm) wooden feet, which they said their father had used to fake the Bigfoot tracks in 1958. Wallace is poorly regarded by many Bigfoot proponents. John Napier wrote, "I do not feel impressed with Mr. Wallace's story" regarding having over 15,000 feet (4,600 m) of film showing Bigfoot.

- 1967: Roger Patterson and Robert Gimlin reported that on October 20 they had captured a purported Sasquatch on film at Bluff Creek, California. This came to be known as the Patterson-Gimlin film. Many years later, Bob Heironimus, an acquaintance of Patterson's, said that he had worn an ape costume for the making of the film. However, Patterson and Gimlin claimed that they sought various experts to examine the film. Patterson claimed to have screened the film for unnamed technicians "in the special effects department at Universal Studios in Hollywood. Their conclusion was: 'We could try (faking it), but we would have to create a completely new system of artificial muscles and find an actor who could be trained to walk like that.

It might be done, but we would have to say that it would be almost impossible.'"

- 2007: On September 16, 2007, hunter Rick Jacobs captured an image of a supposed Sasquatch by using an automatically triggered camera attached to a tree, prompting a spokesperson for the Pennsylvania Game Commission to say that it was probably an image of "a bear with a severe case of mange." The photo was taken near the town of Ridgway, Pennsylvania, in the Allegheny National Forest.

Proposed Explanations For Sightings

Various types of creatures have been suggested to explain both the sightings and what type of creature Bigfoot would be if it existed. The scientific community typically attributes sightings to either hoaxes or misidentification of known animals and their tracks. While cryptozoologists generally explain Bigfoot as an unknown ape, some believers in Bigfoot attribute the phenomenon to UFOs or other paranormal causes.

Misidentification

In 2007, the Pennsylvania Game Commission said that photos the Bigfoot Field Researchers Organization claimed showed a juvenile Bigfoot were probably of a bear with mange. Jeffrey Meldrum, on the other hand, said the limb proportions of the suspected juvenile in question were not bear-like, and stated that he felt they were "more like a chimpanzee."

Hoaxes

Both scientists and Bigfoot believers agree that many of the sightings are hoaxes or misidentified animals.

Bigfoot sightings or footprints are often demonstrably hoaxes. Author Jerome Clark argues that the Jacko Affair, involving an 1884 newspaper report of an apelike creature captured in British Columbia was a hoax. Citing research by John Green, who found that several contemporary British Columbia newspapers regarded the alleged capture as very dubious, Clark notes that the Mainland Guardian of New Westminster, British Columbia, wrote, "Absurdity is written on the face of it."

On July 14, 2005, Tom Biscardi, a long-time Bigfoot enthusiast and CEO of Searching for Bigfoot Inc., appeared on the Coast to Coast AM paranormal radio show and announced that he was "98% sure that his group will be able to capture a Bigfoot which they have been tracking in the Happy Camp, California area."

A month later, Biscardi announced on the same radio show that he had access to a captured Bigfoot and was arranging a pay-per-view event for people to see it. Biscardi appeared on Coast to Coast AM again a few days later to announce that there was no captive Bigfoot. Biscardi blamed an unnamed woman for misleading him and the show's audience for being gullible.

On July 9, 2008, Rick Dyer and Matthew Whitton posted a video to YouTube claiming that they had discovered the body of a dead Sasquatch in a forest in northern Georgia. Tom Biscardi was contacted to investigate. Dyer and Whitton received $50,000 from *Searching for Bigfoo*t, Inc., as a good faith gesture.

The story of the men's claims was covered by many major news networks, including BBC, CNN, ABC News, and Fox News. Soon after a press conference, the alleged Bigfoot body arrived in a block of ice in a freezer with the Searching for Bigfoot team. When the contents were thawed, it was discovered that the hair was not real, the head was hollow, and the feet were rubber. Dyer and Whitton subsequently admitted it was a hoax after being confronted by Steve Kulls, executive director of SquatchDetective.com.

In August 2012, a man in Montana was killed by a car while perpetrating a Bigfoot hoax using a ghillie suit.

In January 2014, Rick Dyer, perpetrator of a previous Bigfoot hoax, claimed to have killed a Bigfoot creature in September 2012 outside of San Antonio, Texas. Dyer claims to have had scientific tests performed on the body, "from DNA tests to 3D optical scans to body scans. It is the real deal. It's Bigfoot and Bigfoot's here, and I shot it and now I'm proving it to the world."

He stated that he intended to take the body, which he has kept in a hidden location, on tour across North America in 2014. To date, he has released only photos of the body and a video showing a few individuals' reactions to seeing it, but none of the tests or scans. He has refused to disclose the test results or provide biological samples, although he has stated that the DNA results, which were done by an undisclosed lab, could not identify any known animal. He stated he would reveal the body and tests on February 9 at a news conference at Washington University, however, the test results are still unavailable. After the Phoenix tour, the body traveled to Houston.

On March 28, 2014, Dyer admitted on his Facebook page that his current "Bigfoot corpse" was another hoax. He paid Chris Russel of Twisted Toy Box to manufacture the prop, which he nicknamed "Hank", from latex, foam and camel hair. Dyer raked in approximately $60,000 from the tour of his second fake Bigfoot corpse. He maintains that he really did kill a Bigfoot, but didn't take the real body on tour for fear it would be stolen.

Gigantopithecus

Bigfoot proponents Grover Krantz and Geoffrey Bourne believed that Bigfoot could be a relict population of Gigantopithecus. Bourne contends that as all Gigantopithecus fossils were found in Asia, and as many species of animals migrated across the Bering land bridge, it is not unreasonable to assume that Gigantopithecus might have as well.

The Gigantopithecus hypothesis is generally considered entirely speculative. Gigantopithecus fossils are not found in the Americas. As the only recovered fossils are of mandibles and teeth, there is some uncertainty about Gigantopithecus's locomotion. Krantz has argued, based on his extrapolation of the shape of its mandible, that Gigantopithecus blacki could have been bipedal. However, the relevant part of mandible is not present in any fossils. The mainstream view is that Gigantopithecus was a quadruped, and it has been argued that Gigantopithecus's enormous mass would have made it difficult for it to adopt a bipedal gait.

Matt Cartmill presents another problem with the Gigantopithecus hypothesis: "The trouble with this account is that Gigantopithecus was not a hominin and maybe not even a crown-group hominoid; yet the physical evidence implies that Bigfoot is an upright biped with buttocks and a long, stout, permanently adducted hallux. These are hominin autapomorphies, not found in other mammals or other bipeds. It seems unlikely that Gigantopithecus would have evolved these uniquely hominin traits in parallel."

Bernard G. Campbell wrote: "That Gigantopithecus is in fact extinct has been questioned by those who believe it survives as the Yeti of the Himalayas and the Sasquatch of the north-west American coast. But the evidence for these creatures is not convincing."

Extinct Hominidae

A species of Paranthropus, such as Paranthropus robustus, with its crested skull and bipedal gait, was suggested by primatologist John Napier and anthropologist

Gordon Strasenburg as a possible candidate for Bigfoot's identity, despite the fact that fossils of Paranthropus are found only in Africa.

Michael Rugg, of the Bigfoot Discovery Museum, presented a comparison between human, Gigantopithecus and Meganthropus skulls (reconstructions made by Grover Krantz) in episodes 131 and 132 of the Bigfoot Discovery Museum Show. He favorably compares a modern tooth suspected of coming from a Bigfoot to the Meganthropus fossil teeth, noting the worn enamel on the occlusal surface. The Meganthropus fossils originated from Asia, and the tooth was found near Santa Cruz, California.

Some suggest Neanderthal, Homo erectus, or Homo heidelbergensis to be the creature, but no remains of any of those species have been found in the Americas.

Scientific View

The scientific community discounts the existence of Bigfoot, as there is no evidence supporting the survival of such a large, prehistoric ape-like creature. The evidence that does exist points more towards a hoax or delusion than to sightings of a genuine creature. In a 1996 USA Today article, Washington State zoologist John Crane said, *"There is no such thing as Bigfoot. No data other than material that's clearly been fabricated has ever been presented."* In addition to the lack of evidence, scientists cite the fact that Bigfoot is alleged to live in regions unusual for a large, nonhuman primate, i.e., temperate latitudes in the northern hemisphere; all recognized apes are found in the tropics of Africa and Asia.

The subject of Bigfoot is not considered an area of credible science and there have been a limited number of formal scientific studies of Bigfoot.

Supposed evidence like the 1967 Patterson-Gimlin film has provided "no supportive data of any scientific value".

As with other proposed megafauna cryptids, climate and food supply issues would make such a creature's survival in reported habitats unlikely. Great apes are not found in the fossil record in the Americas, and no Bigfoot remains are known to have been found. Scientific consensus is that the breeding population of such an animal would be so large that it would account for many more purported sightings than currently occur, making the existence of such an animal an almost certain impossibility. In the 1970s, when Bigfoot "experts" were frequently given high-profile media coverage, the scientific community generally avoided lending credence to the theories by debating them.

Researchers

Ivan Sanderson and Bernard Heuvelmans have spent parts of their career searching for Bigfoot. Later scientists who researched the topic included Carleton S. Coon, George Allen Agogino and William Charles Osman Hill, although they came to no definite conclusions and later drifted from this research.

Jeffrey Meldrum has said that the fossil remains of an ancient giant ape called Gigantopithecus could turn out to be ancestors of today's commonly known Bigfoot, but this claim hasn't been accepted by the scientific community. John Napier asserts that the scientific community's attitude towards Bigfoot stems primarily from insufficient evidence. Other scientists who have shown varying degrees of interest in the legend are David Daegling, George Schaller, Russell Mittermeier, Daris Swindler, Esteban Sarmiento, and Carleton S. Coon.

Jane Goodall, in a September 27, 2002, interview on National Public Radio's "Science Friday", expressed her ideas about the existence of Bigfoot. First stating "I'm sure they exist", she later went on to say, chuckling, "Well, I'm a romantic, so I always wanted them to exist", and finally: "You know, why isn't there a body? I can't answer that, and maybe they don't exist, but I want them to."[87] In 2012, Goodall said, "I'm fascinated and would actually love them to exist."

Formal Studies

The first scientific study of available evidence was conducted by primatologist John Napier and published in his book, Bigfoot: The Yeti and Sasquatch in Myth and Reality, in 1973.[89] Napier wrote that if a conclusion is to be reached based on scant extant "'hard' evidence," science must declare "Bigfoot does not exist."[90] However, he found it difficult to entirely reject thousands of alleged tracks, "scattered over 125,000 square miles" or to dismiss all "the many hundreds" of eyewitness accounts. Napier concluded, "I am convinced that Sasquatch exists, but whether it is all it is cracked up to be is another matter altogether. There must be something in north-west America that needs explaining, and that something leaves man-like footprints."

In 1974, the National Wildlife Federation funded a field study seeking Bigfoot evidence. No formal federation members were involved and the study made no notable discoveries.

Beginning in the late 1970s, physical anthropologist Grover Krantz published several articles and four book-length treatments of Sasquatch. However, his work was found to contain multiple scientific failings including falling for hoaxes.

A study published in for the Journal of Biogeography in 2009 by J.D. Lozier et al. used ecological niche modeling on reported sightings of Bigfoot, using their locations to infer Bigfoot's preferred ecological parameters. They found a very close match with the ecological parameters of the American black bear, Ursus Americanus. They also note that an upright bear looks much like Bigfoot's purported appearance and consider it highly improbable that two species should have very similar ecological preferences, concluding that Bigfoot sightings are likely sightings of black bears.

Bigfoot Claims

After what The Huffington Post described as "a five-year study of purported Bigfoot (also known as Sasquatch) DNA samples," Texas veterinarian Melba Ketchum and her team announced that they had found proof that the Sasquatch "is a human relative that arose approximately 15,000 years ago as a hybrid cross of modern Homo sapiens with an unknown primate species."

Ketchum called for this to be recognized officially, saying that "Government at all levels must recognize them as an indigenous people and immediately protect their human and Constitutional rights against those who would see in their physical and cultural differences a 'license' to hunt, trap, or kill them."

Failing to find a scientific journal that would publish their results, Ketchum announced on February 13, 2013 that their research had been published in the DeNovo Journal of Science. The Huffington Post discovered that the journal's domain had been registered anonymously only nine days before the announcement. The only edition of DeNovo was listed as Volume 1, Issue 1, and its only content was the Bigfoot research.

One Expedition

In 2013 I made a trip to Dulce, New Mexico, which is, among other things a home for the Sasquatch. I conducted a number of interviews with individuals who had seen these creatures. The stories that I collected are amazing. A series of videos will be released later which discuss these events.

CHAPTER SEVENTEEN

EL CHUPACABRA

The Chupacabra (Spanish pronunciation: [tʃupaˈkaβɾa], from chupar "to suck" and cabra "goat", literally "goat sucker") is a legendary cryptid rumored to inhabit parts of the Americas, with the first sightings reported in Puerto Rico. The name comes from the animal's reported habit of attacking and drinking the blood of livestock, especially goats.

Physical descriptions of the creature vary. It is purportedly a heavy creature, the size of a small bear, with a row of spines reaching from the neck to the base of the tail.

Eyewitness sightings have been claimed as early as 1995 in Puerto Rico, and have since been reported as far north as Maine, and as far south as Chile, and even being spotted outside the Americas in countries like Russia and

The Philippines, but many of the reports have been disregarded as uncorroborated or lacking evidence. Sightings in northern Mexico and the southern United States have been verified as canids afflicted by mange. Biologists and wildlife management officials view the Chupacabra as a contemporary legend.

History

The first reported attacks occurred in March 1995 in Puerto Rico. In this attack, eight sheep were discovered dead, each with three puncture wounds in the chest area and completely drained of blood. A few months later, in August, an eyewitness, Madelyne Tolentino, reported seeing the creature in the Puerto Rican town of Canóvanas, when as many as 150 farm animals and pets were reportedly killed. In 1975, similar killings in the small town of Moca were attributed to El Vampiro de Moca (The Vampire of Moca). Initially, it was suspected that the killings were committed by a Satanic cult; later more killings were reported around the island, and many farms reported loss of animal life. Each of the animals was reported to have had its body bled dry through a series of small circular incisions.

Puerto Rican comedian and entrepreneur Silverio Pérez is credited with coining the term Chupacabra soon after the first incidents were reported in the press. Shortly after the first reported incidents in Puerto Rico, other animal deaths were reported in other countries, such as the Dominican Republic, Argentina, Bolivia, Chile, Colombia, Honduras, El Salvador, Nicaragua, Panama, Peru, Brazil, United States, and Mexico.

Possible Origin

A five-year investigation by Benjamin Radford concluded that the description given by the original eyewitness in Puerto Rico, Madelyne Tolentino, was based on the creature Sil in the science-fiction horror film Species. The alien creature Sil is nearly identical to Tolentino's Chupacabra eyewitness account and she had seen the movie before her report: "It was a creature that looked like the Chupacabra, with spines on its back and all. The resemblance to the Chupacabra was really impressive," Tolentino reported.

Radford revealed that Tolentino "believed that the creatures and events she saw in Species were actually happening in reality in Puerto Rico at the time," and therefore concludes that "the most important Chupacabra description cannot be trusted." This, Radford believes, seriously undermines the credibility of the Chupacabra as a real animal.

In addition, the reports of blood-sucking by the Chupacabra were never confirmed by a necropsy, the only way to conclude that the animal was drained of blood. An analysis by a veterinarian of 300 reported victims of the Chupacabra found that they had not been bled dry.

Radford divided the Chupacabra reports into two categories: the reports from Puerto Rico and Latin America where animals were attacked and it is supposed their blood was extracted; the reports in the United States of mammals, mostly dogs and coyotes with mange, that people call "Chupacabra" due to their unusual appearance.

In late October 2010, University of Michigan biologist Barry O'Connor concluded that all the Chupacabra reports in the United States were simply coyotes infected with the parasite Sarcoptes scabiei, the symptoms of which would explain most of the features of the Chupacabra: they would be left with little fur, thickened skin, and rank odor. O'Connor theorized the attacks on goats occurred "because these animals are greatly weakened, they're going to have a hard time hunting. So they may be forced into attacking livestock because it's easier than running down a rabbit or a deer."

Although several witnesses came to the conclusion that the attacks could not be the work of dogs or coyotes because they had not eaten the victim, this conclusion is incorrect. Both dogs and coyotes can kill and not consume the prey, either because they are inexperienced, or due to injury or difficulty in killing the prey. The prey can survive the attack and die afterwards from internal bleeding or circulatory shock. The presence of two holes in the neck, corresponding with the canine teeth, is to be expected since this is the only way that most land carnivores have to catch their prey.

Reported Sightings

Numerous sightings of the creature were reported during the mid-1990s in Mexico, the U.S. Southwest and China. The first reported sightings were in Puerto Rico, US, where more than 200 original reports were made in 1995.

In July 2004, a rancher near San Antonio, Texas, killed a hairless dog-like creature which was attacking his livestock. This animal, initially given the name the Elmendorf Beast, was later determined by DNA assay conducted at University of California, Davis to be a coyote with demodectic or sarcoptic mange. In October 2004, two more carcasses were found in the same area. Biologists in Texas examined samples from the two carcasses and determined they were also coyotes suffering from very severe cases of mange.

In Coleman, Texas, a farmer named Reggie Lagow caught an animal in a trap he set up after the deaths of a number of his chickens and turkeys. The animal was described as resembling a mix of hairless dog, rat, and kangaroo. Lagow provided the animal to Texas Parks and Wildlife officials for identification, but Lagow reported in a September 17, 2006, phone interview with John Adolfi, founder of the Lost World Museum, that the "critter was caught on a Tuesday and thrown out in Thursday's trash."

In April 2006, MosNews reported that the Chupacabra was spotted in Russia for the first time. Reports from Central Russia beginning in March 2005 tell of a beast that kills animals and sucks out their blood. 32 turkeys were killed and drained overnight. Reports later came from neighboring villages when 30 sheep were killed and had their blood drained. Finally, eyewitnesses were able to describe the Chupacabra. In May 2006, experts were determined to track the animal down. According to Russian paranormal researcher Vadim Chernobrov, the territory allegedly frequented by Chupacabra lies in the Kharkov region of Ukraine and neighboring regions of Russia, but also in parts of Belarus and Poland.

Recently the reports appeared of Chupacabra-like attacks in the Moscow region of Russia with dozens of birds and animals found bloodless, with strange incisions. At least twice the mysterious kangaroo-like creature ("with a crocodile head") attacked humans, causing no serious damage, though. According to Chernobrov, the two extraordinary things about the Chupacabras' ways are that the thing leaves a 'vanishing' line of footprints, looking as if it takes off as a bird, and also it tends occasionally to assort its victim's bodies 'aesthetically', often by color and size, or build pyramids with killed bodies.

In mid-August 2006, Michelle O'Donnell of Turner, Maine, described an "evil looking" rodent-like animal with fangs that had been found dead alongside a road. The animal was apparently struck by a car, and was unidentifiable. Photographs were taken and witness reports seem to be in relative agreement that the creature was canine in appearance, but in widely published photos seemed unlike any dog or wolf in the area. Photos from other angles seem to show a chow or akita mixed-breed dog. It was reported that "the carcass was picked clean by vultures before experts could examine it". For years, residents of Maine have reported a mysterious creature and a string of dog maulings.

In May 2007, a series of reports on national Colombia news reported more than 300 dead sheep in the region of Boyacá, and the capture of a possible specimen to be analyzed by zoologists at the National University of Colombia.

In August 2007, Phylis Canion found three animals in Cuero, Texas. She and her neighbors reported to have discovered three strange animal carcasses outside Canion's property. She took photographs of the carcasses and preserved the head of one in her freezer before turning it over for DNA analysis. Canion reported that nearly 30 chickens on her farm had been exsanguinated over a period of years, a factor which led her to connect the carcasses with the Chupacabra legend. State Mammologist John Young estimated that the animal in Canion's pictures was a Gray Fox suffering from an extreme case of mange. In November 2007, biology researchers at Texas State University–San Marcos determined from DNA samples that the suspicious animal was a coyote.

The coyote, however, had grayish-blue, mostly hairless skin and large fanged teeth, attributes which caused it to appear different from a normal coyote. Additional skin samples were taken to attempt to determine the cause of the hair loss.

On January 11, 2008, a sighting was reported at the province of Capes in the Philippines. Some of the residents from the barangay believed that it was the Chupacabra that killed eight chickens. The owner of the chickens saw a dog-like animal attacking his chickens.

On August 8, 2008, a DeWitt County deputy, Brandon Riedel, filmed an unidentifiable animal along back roads near Cuero, Texas, on his dashboard camera. The animal was about the size of a coyote but was hairless with a long snout, short front legs and long back legs. However, Reiter's boss, Sheriff Jode Zavesky, believes it may be the same species of coyote identified by Texas State University–San Marcos researchers in November 2007.

The video footage was shown on an April 2011 episode of the SyFy television series Fact or Faked: Paranormal Files where an investigative team tried to recreate the dashboard video footage using a miniature horse and a Mexican Hairless Dog (both of which were bred locally). Neither test animal matched the creature in the video. The team had also tested a DNA sample taken from an alleged carcass of one of the creatures found by a local rancher and later identified as being a hybrid wolf/coyote.

In September 2009, CNN aired a report showing close-up video footage of an unidentified dead animal. The same CNN report stated that locals have begun speculating the possibility that this might be a Chupacabra. A Blanco, Texas, taxidermist reported that he received the body from a former student whose cousin had discovered the animal in his barn, where it had succumbed to poison left out for rodents. The taxidermist expressed his belief that this is a genetically mutated coyote.

On September 18, 2009, taxidermist Jerry Ayer sold the Blanco Texas Chupacabra to the Lost World Museum. The museum, as reported in the Syracuse Post Standard on 9/26/09, is placing the creature on display as it works with an unnamed university to have the remains tested.

In July 2010, there were reports of Chupacabras being shot dead by animal control officers in Hood County, Texas. A second creature was also reportedly spotted and killed several miles away. However, an officer of Hood County animal control said Texas A&M University scientists conducted tests and identified the corpse as a "coyote-dog hybrid" with signs of mange and internal parasites. The second reported Chupacabra, shot July 9 about 8 miles south of Cresson, was eaten by vultures before it could be taken for testing.

On December 18, 2010, in Nelson County, Kentucky, Mark Cothren shot and killed an animal that he could not recognize and feared. Many pictures of the Chupacabra were taken and the story was well documented by various news organizations. Cothren described the creature as having large ears, whiskers, a long tail, and about the size of a house cat. Cothren says he spoke with the Kentucky Department of Fish and Wildlife Resources and handed over the preserved animal for further analysis.

On July 4, 2011, Jack (Jeff) Crabtree, of Lake Jackson, Texas, reported seeing a Chupacabra in his back yard. At first, Crabtree stood firm on his original theory of the Chupacabra, but after the local newspaper and several other media reporters wrote his story on July 11, he quickly backed down, agreeing with wildlife experts that it was most likely a coyote with mange.

"It was a spoof or a practical joke," Crabtree said. "...I really didn't believe it."

His story appeared on CNN, as well as MSNBC. On July 15, 2011, local authorities caught what Crabtree saw. Experts confirmed that the animal was definitely a coyote with mange.

On September 17, 2013, the Fox 2 News affiliate in Saint Louis, Missouri, posted on its website a report of two sightings. In the first, a woman spotted a "small grey dog-like animal" near the front gate of the Old Lake Hill Speedway in Saint Louis. A week previously, a hunter claimed to have killed a Chupacabra while "coon hunting". The Mississippi Department of Wildlife said that it was a dog with mange.

A Texan couple who reside on a ranch in Victoria County, Texas informed the media that they had shot and killed a Chupacabra on their property during the evening of February 23, 2014. A wildlife biologist with the Texas Parks and Wildlife organization also spoke with the media and stated: "I've seen squirrels, raccoons and coyotes in this area with the same features. They're [Chupacabra] a mythical creature that most people see, but what it really is sarcoptic mange which is caused by a mite that bites the animal and it can be on any mammal - dogs, cats, coyotes foxes, and humans can get another version of it as well."

On April 3, 2014, a Texan couple claimed to have captured a Chupacabra in Ratcliffe, Texas on March 29, 2014 Livescience's Benjamin Radford suggested the animal is a raccoon suffering from sarcoptic mange.

Appearance

The most common description of the Chupacabra is that of a reptile-like creature, said to have leathery or scaly greenish-gray skin and sharp spines or quills running down its back. It is said to be approximately 3 to 4 feet (1 to 1.2 m) high, and stands and hops in a fashion similar to that of a kangaroo.

Another less common description of the Chupacabra is of a strange breed of wild dog. This form is mostly hairless and has a pronounced spinal ridge, unusually pronounced eye sockets, fangs, and claws. Unlike conventional predators, the Chupacabra is said to drain all of the animal's blood (and sometimes organs) usually through three holes in the shape of an upside-down triangle or through one or two holes.

The Name

The name Chupacabra can be translated as "goat-sucker". It is known as both Chupacabras and Chupacabra throughout the Americas, with the former being the original word, and the latter a regularization of it. The name in Spanish can be preceded by a singular masculine article (el Chupacabras), or the plural masculine article (los Chupacabras).

Related Legends

A popular legend in New Orleans concerns a popular lovers' lane called Grunch Road, which was said to be inhabited by "grunches", creatures similar in appearance to the Chupacabra.

The Peuchen of Chile also share similarities in their supposed habits, but instead of being dog-like they are described as winged snakes. This legend may have originated from the vampire bat, an animal endemic to the region.

In the Philippines, another legendary creature called the Sigbin shares many of the same descriptions as the Chupacabra. The recent discovery of the cat-fox in Southeast Asia suggests that it could also have been simply sightings of this once unknown animal.

CHAPTER EIGHTEEN

POLTERGEISTS

In folklore and parapsychology, a poltergeist is a type of ghost or other supernatural being supposedly responsible for physical disturbances such as loud noises and objects moved around or destroyed. Most accounts of poltergeists describe movement or levitation of objects, such as furniture and cutlery, or noises such as knocking on doors. Poltergeists have also been claimed to be capable of pinching, biting, hitting and tripping people.

Poltergeists occupy numerous niches in cultural folklore, and have traditionally been described as troublesome spirits who haunt a particular person instead of a specific location. Such alleged poltergeist manifestations have been reported in many cultures and countries including the United States, Japan, Brazil, Australia, and most European nations, with early accounts dating back to the 1st century.

The Name

The word poltergeist comes from the German words poltern ("to make sound") and Geist ("ghost" and "spirit"), and the term itself roughly translates as "noisy ghost" or "noise-ghost".

Science

Many claimed poltergeist events have proved on investigation to be pranks. According to research in anomalistic psychology claims of poltergeist activity can be explained by psychological factors such as illusion, memory lapses and wishful thinking. A study (Lange and Houran, 1998) wrote that poltergeist experiences are delusions "resulting from the affective and cognitive dynamics of percipients' interpretation of ambiguous stimuli".

Attempts have also been made to explain scientifically poltergeist disturbances that have not been traced to fraud or psychological factors. The psychical investigator Guy William Lambert proposed a geophysical explanation for poltergeist activity which results from the activity of underground water and other factors. According to Lambert many reported poltergeist incidents can be accounted for by physical causes such as "subterranean rivers, tidal patterns, geological factors and shifts in the house foundation, and climate changes." His theory was that an underground water course may flow under "haunted" locations and that after heavy rainfall the stream could cause structural movement of the property, possibly causing the house to vibrate and move objects.

David Turner, a retired physical chemist, suggested that ball lightning, another phenomenon, could cause inanimate objects to move erratically.

Skeptics such as Milbourne Christopher have found that some cases of poltergeist activity can be attributed to unusual air currents, such as a 1957 case on Cape Cod where downdrafts from an uncovered chimney became strong enough to blow a mirror off of a wall, overturn chairs and knock things off shelves.

Skeptic Joe Nickell says that claimed poltergeist incidents typically originate from "an individual who is motivated to cause mischief". According to Nickell:

"In the typical poltergeist outbreak, small objects are hurled through the air by unseen forces, furniture is overturned, or other disturbances occur -- usually just what could be accomplished by a juvenile trickster determined to plague credulous adults."

Ken Hudnall

Nickell writes that reports are often exaggerated by credulous witnesses.

"Time and again in other "poltergeist" outbreaks, witnesses have re-ported an object leaping from its resting place supposedly on its own, when it is likely that the perpetrator had secretly ob-tained the object sometime earlier and waited for an opportunity to fling it, even from outside the room—thus supposedly proving he or she was innocent."

Other investigators have postulated that psychopathology or aggression in the subjects themselves may be responsible for the action of movement of objects in poltergeist cases. Nandor Fodor proposed that poltergeist disturbances are caused by human agents suffering from some form of emotional stress or tension and compared reports of poltergeist activity to hysterical conversion symptoms resulting from emotional tension of the subject.

Paranormal

Poltergeist activity has often been believed to be the work of malicious spirits. According to Allan Kardec, the founder of Spiritism, poltergeists are manifestations of disembodied spirits of low level, belonging to the sixth class of the third order. They are believed to be closely associated with the elements (fire, air, water, earth).

The parapsychologist William Roll wrote that poltergeist activity can be explained by psychokinesis.

Some cultures attribute poltergeist activity to the souls of deceased relatives of the family or person: dybbuks in Jewish mythology for example, are often described as possessing characteristics of a poltergeist.

Famous poltergeist cases

- Borley Rectory (1937) investigated by Harry Price who called it "the most haunted house in England".
- Rosenheim Poltergeist (1967) investigated by Hans Bender who claimed that a law firm located in Rosenheim in southern Germany experienced disruption of electricity and telephone lines, swinging lamps, and the rotation of a framed picture caused by a 19-year-old secretary who he alleged was "a typical poltergeist."
- The Black Monk of Pontefract
- The Enfield Poltergeist (1977)
- Drummer of Tedworth (1662).
- The Bell Witch of Tennessee (1817–1872)
- Great Amherst Mystery (1878–79)

- Epworth Rectory (1716-1717)
- Gef the Talking Mongoose (1931)
- Robbie Mannheim (1949), claimed to be demonically possessed after using an Ouija board.
- The Thornton Road poltergeist of Birmingham (1981)
- Angelique Cottin (ca. 1846)
- Tina Resch (1984)
- "The Stone-Throwing Spook of Little Dixie" (1995)
- The Canneto di Caronia fires poltergeist (2004–5)
- The Miami Poltergeist (2008)
- Barnsley near Sheffield in England (2009)
- "Jim", the Coventry poltergeist (2011). In a series of articles in March 2011, The Sun reported that Lisa Manning and her children believed they were being disturbed by a poltergeist. Derek Acorah visited Manning's home and claimed that he was able to "communicate with the spirit."

CHAPTER NINETEEN

ALIEN ABDUCTIONS

The terms alien abduction or abduction phenomenon describe "subjectively real memories of being taken secretly against one's will by apparently nonhuman entities and subjected to complex physical and psychological procedures". People claiming to have been abducted are usually called "abductees" or "experiencers".

Due to a paucity of objective physical evidence, most scientists and mental health professionals dismiss the phenomenon as "deception, suggestibility (fantasy-proneness, hypnotizability, and false memory syndrome), personality, sleep paralysis, psychopathology, psychodynamics [and] environmental factors". However, the late Prof. John E. Mack, a respected Harvard University psychiatrist, devoted a substantial amount of time to investigating such cases and eventually concluded that the only phenomenon in psychiatry that adequately explained the patients' symptoms in several of the most compelling cases was posttraumatic stress disorder. As he noted at the time, this would imply that the patient genuinely believed that the remembered frightening incident had really occurred.

Skeptic Robert Sheaffer sees similarity between the aliens depicted in early science fiction films, in particular, Invaders From Mars, and some of those reported to have actually abducted people.

Typical claims involve being subjected to a forced medical examination that emphasizes their reproductive system. Abductees sometimes claim to have been warned against environmental abuse and the dangers of nuclear weapons. While many of these claimed encounters are described as terrifying, some have been viewed as pleasurable or transformative.

The first alleged alien abduction claim to be widely publicized was the Betty and Barney Hill abduction in 1961. Reports of the abduction phenomenon have been made around the world, but are most common in English speaking countries, especially the United States. The contents of the abduction narrative often seem to vary with the home culture of the alleged abductee.

Alien abductions have been the subject of conspiracy theories and science fiction storylines (notably The X-Files) that have speculated on stealth technology required if the phenomenon were real, the motivations for secrecy, and that alien implants could be a possible form of physical evidence.

Overview

CUFOS Definition of an Abductee

1. A person must be taken:
2. Against his or her will
3. From terrestrial surroundings
4. By non-human beings.
5. The beings must take the person to:

- An enclosed place
- Not terrestrial in appearance
- Assumed or known to be an alien spacecraft by the witness.

6. In this place, the person must either:

- Be subjected to an examination,
- Engage in communication (verbal or telepathic),
- Or both.

7. These experiences may be remembered:

- Consciously

- Or through methods of focused concentration such as hypnosis.

Mainstream scientists reject claims that the phenomenon literally occurs as reported. However, there is little doubt that many apparently stable persons who report alien abductions believe their experiences were real. As reported in the Harvard University Gazette in 1992, Dr. John E. Mack investigated over 800 claimed abductees and "spent countless therapeutic hours with these individuals only to find that what struck him was the 'ordinariness' of the population, including a restaurant owner, several secretaries, a prison guard, college students, a university administrator, and several homemakers ... 'The majority of abductees do not appear to be deluded, confabulating, lying, self-dramatizing, or suffering from a clear mental illness,' he maintained."

"While psychopathology is indicated in some isolated alien abduction cases," Stuart Appelle et al. confirmed, "assessment by both clinical examination and standardized tests has shown that, as a group, abduction experients are not different from the general population in term of psychopathology prevalence."[10] Other experts who have argued that abductees' mental health is no better or worse than average include psychologists John Wilson and Rima Laibow, and psychotherapist David Gotlib.

Some abduction reports are quite detailed. An entire subculture has developed around the subject, with support groups and a detailed mythos explaining the reasons for abductions: The various aliens (Greys, Reptilians, "Nordics" and so on) are said to have specific roles, origins, and motivations. Abduction claimants do not always attempt to explain the phenomenon, but some take independent research interest in it themselves and explain the lack of greater awareness of alien abduction as the result of either extraterrestrial or governmental interest in cover-up.

History

As noted below, the Antonio Vilas Boas case (1957) and the Hill abduction (1961) were the first cases of UFO abduction to earn widespread attention.

Though these two cases are sometimes viewed as the earliest abductions, skeptic Peter Rogerson notes this assertion is incorrect: the Hill and Boas abductions, he contends, were only the first "canonical" abduction cases, establishing a template that later abductees and researchers would refine but rarely deviate from. Additionally,

Rogerson notes purported abductions were cited contemporaneously at least as early as 1954 and that "the growth of the abduction stories is a far more tangled affair than the 'entirely unpredisposed' official history would have us believe." (The phrase "entirely unpredisposed" appeared in folklorist Thomas E. Bullard's study of alien abduction; he argued that alien abductions as reported in the 1970s and 1980s had little precedent in folklore or fiction.)

Paleo-abductions

While "alien abduction" did not achieve widespread attention until the 1960s, there were many similar stories circulating decades earlier. These early abduction-like accounts have been dubbed "paleo-abductions" by UFO researcher Jerome Clark.

In an 1897 edition of the Stockton, California Daily Mail, Colonel H. G. Shaw claimed he and a friend were harassed by three tall, slender humanoids whose bodies were covered with a fine, downy hair who tried to kidnap the pair.

Rogerson writes that the 1955 publication of Harold T. Wilkins's Flying Saucers Uncensored declared that Karl Hunrath and Wilbur Wilkinson, who had claimed they were contacted by aliens, had disappeared under mysterious circumstances; Wilkins reported speculation that the duo were the victims of "alleged abduction by flying saucers".

Contactees

The UFO contactees of the 1950s claimed to have contacted aliens, and the substance of contactee narratives - in which the beings express the intent to help mankind stop nuclear testing and prevent the otherwise inevitable destruction of the human race.

Two landmark cases

An early alien abduction claim occurred in the mid-1950s with the Antonio Vilas Boas case, which did not receive much attention until several years later.

Widespread publicity was generated by the Betty and Barney Hill abduction case of 1961, culminating in a made-for-television film broadcast in 1975 (starring James Earl Jones and Estelle Parsons) dramatizing the events. The Hill incident was probably the prototypical abduction case and was perhaps the first in which the claimant described beings that later became widely known as the Greys and in which the beings were said to explicitly identify an extraterrestrial origin.

Later Developments

Dr. R. Leo Sprinkle (University of Wyoming psychologist) became interested in the abduction phenomenon in the 1960s. For some years, he was probably the only academic figure devoting any time to studying or researching abduction accounts. Sprinkle became convinced of the phenomenon's actuality, and was perhaps the first to suggest a link between abductions and cattle mutilation. Eventually Sprinkle came to believe that he had been abducted by aliens in his youth; he was forced from his job in 1989. (Bryan, 145fn)

Budd Hopkins — an accomplished painter and sculptor — had been interested in UFOs for some years. In the 1970s he became interested in abduction reports, and began using hypnosis to extract more details of dimly remembered events. Hopkins soon became a figurehead of the growing abductee subculture. (Schnabel 1994)

The 1980s brought a major degree of mainstream attention to the subject. Works by Budd Hopkins, novelist Whitley Strieber, historian David M. Jacobs and psychiatrist John E. Mack presented alien abduction as a genuine phenomenon (Schnabel 1994). Also of note in the 1980s was the publication of folklorist Dr. Thomas E.

Bullard's comparative analysis of nearly 300 alleged abductees.

With Hopkins, Jacobs and Mack, accounts of alien abduction became a prominent aspect of ufology. There had been earlier abduction reports (the Hills being the best known), but they were believed to be few and far between, and saw rather little attention from ufology (and even less attention from mainstream professionals or academics). Jacobs and Hopkins argued that alien abduction was far more common than earlier suspected; they estimate that tens of thousands (or more) North Americans had been taken by unexplained beings (Schnabel 1994).

Furthermore, Jacobs and Hopkins argued that there was an elaborate process underway in which aliens were attempting to create human–alien hybrids, though the motives for this effort were unknown. There had been anecdotal reports of phantom pregnancy related to UFO encounters at least as early as the 1960s, but Budd Hopkins and especially David M. Jacobs were instrumental in popularizing the idea of widespread, systematic interbreeding efforts on the part of the alien intruders.

The descriptions of alien encounters as researched and presented by Hopkins, Jacob and Mack were similar, with slight differences in each researcher's emphasis; the process of selective citation of abductee interviews that supported these variations were sometimes criticized, by though abductees who presented their own accounts directly, such as Whitley Strieber, fared no better.

The involvement of Jacobs and Mack marked something of a sea change in the abduction studies. Their efforts were controversial (both men saw some degree of damage to their professional reputations), but to other observers, Jacobs and Mack brought a degree of respectability to the subject.

John E. Mack

Matheson writes that "if Jacobs's credentials were impressive," then those of Harvard psychiatrist John E. Mack might seem "impeccable" in comparison. (Matheson, 251) Mack was a well-known, highly esteemed psychiatrist, author of over 150 scientific articles and winner of the Pulitzer Prize for his biography of T. E. Lawrence. Mack became interested in the phenomenon in the late 1980s, interviewing over 800 people, and eventually writing two books on the subject.

In June 1992, Mack and the physicist David E. Pritchard organized a five-day conference at MIT to discuss and debate the abduction phenomenon. The conference attracted a wide range of professionals, representing a variety of perspectives. As their thanks for their efforts to focus a modest level of serious scientific attention on the perplexing "abduction" phenomenon by organizing this conference, Mack and Jacobs were awarded an Ig Nobel Prize in 1993.

Writer C. D. B. Bryan attended the conference, initially intending to gather information for a short humorous article for The New Yorker. While attending the conference, however, Bryan's view of the subject changed, and he wrote a serious, open-minded book on the phenomenon, additionally interviewing many abductees, skeptics, and proponents.

Abductees

The precise number of alleged abductees is uncertain. One of the earliest studies of abductions found 1,700 claimants, while contested surveys argued that 5–6 percent of the general population might have been abducted.

Demographics

In a study investigating the motivations of the alleged abductors, Jenny Randles found that in each of the

4 cases out of 50 total where the experiencer was over 40 years of age or more, they were rejected by the aliens for "what they (the experiencers) usually inferred to be a medical reason." Randles concludes "the abduction is essentially a young person's experience."

Given the reproductive focus of the alleged abductions it is not surprising that one man reported being rejected because he had undergone a vasectomy. It could also be partially because people over the age of 40 are less likely to have "hormonic" or reproductive activity going on.

Although abduction and other UFO-related reports are usually made by adults, sometimes young children report similar experiences. These child-reports often feature very specific details in common with reports of abduction made by adults, including the circumstances, narrative, entities and aftermaths of the alleged occurrences. Often these young abductees have family members who have reported having abduction experiences. Family involvement in the military or a residence near a military base is also common amongst child abduction claimants.

Mental Health

As a category, some studies show that abductees have psychological characteristics that render their testimony suspect, while others show that "as a group, abduction experients are not different from the general population in term of psychopathology prevalence".

Dr. Elizabeth Slater conducted a blind study of nine abduction claimants and found them to be prone to "mildly paranoid thinking," nightmares and having a weak sexual identity, while Dr. Richard McNally of Harvard Medical School concluded in a similar study of 10 abductees that "none of them was suffering from any sort of psychiatric illness."

Paranormal

Alleged abductees are seen by many pro-abduction researchers to have a higher incidence of non-abduction related paranormal events and abilities. Following an abduction experience, these paranormal abilities and occurrences sometimes seem to become more pronounced. According to investigator Benton Jamison, abduction experiencers who report UFO sightings that should have been, but are not, reported by independent corroborating witnesses often seem to "be 'psychic personalities' in the sense of Jan Ehrenwald."

Psychic Medium Danielle Egnew recounted multiple abduction experiences in her 2012 book <u>True Tales of the Truly Weird</u>, greatly detailing communication, technology and abduction methods of more than one alien race.

Miscellaneous

According to Yvonne Smith, some alleged abductees test positive for lupus, despite not showing any symptoms.

Although different cases vary in detail (sometimes significantly), some UFO researchers, such as folklorist Thomas E. Bullard argue that there is a broad, fairly consistent sequence and description of events that make up the typical "close encounter of the fourth kind" (a popular but unofficial designation building on Dr. J. Allen Hynek's classifying terminology). Though the features outlined below are often reported, there is some disagreement as to exactly how often they actually occur.

Bullard argues most abduction accounts feature the following events. They generally follow the sequence noted below, though not all abductions feature all the events:

- 1.   Capture. The abductee is somehow rendered incapable of resisting, and taken from terrestrial surroundings to an apparent alien spacecraft.

- 2.   Examination and Procedures. Invasive physiological and psychological procedures, and on occasion simulated behavioral situations, training & testing, or sexual liaisons.

- 3.   Conference. The abductors communicate with the abductee or direct them to interact with specific individuals for some purpose, typically telepathically but sometimes using the abductee's native language.

- 4.   Tour. The abductees are given a tour of their captors' vessel, though this is disputed by some researchers who consider this definition a confabulation of intent when just apparently being taken around to multiple places inside the ship.

- 5.   Loss of Time. Abductees often rapidly forget the majority of their experience, either as a result of fear, medical intervention, or both.

- 6. Return. The abductees are returned to earth, occasionally in a different location from where they were allegedly taken or with new injuries or disheveled clothing.

- 7. Theophany. Coinciding with their immediate return, abductees may have a profound sense of love, a "high" similar to those induced by certain drugs, or a "mystical experience", accompanied by a feeling of oneness with God, the universe, or their abductors. Whether this is the result of a metaphysical change, Stockholm syndrome, or prior medical tampering is often not scrutinized by the abductees at the time.

- 8. Aftermath. The abductee must cope with the psychological, physical, and social effects of the experience.

When describing the "abduction scenario", David M. Jacobs says:

The entire abduction event is precisely orchestrated. All the procedures are predetermined. There is no standing around and deciding what to do next. The beings are task-oriented and there is no indication whatsoever that we have been able to find of any aspect of their lives outside of performing the abduction procedures.

Capture

Abduction claimants report unusual feelings preceding the onset of an abduction experience. These feelings manifest as a compulsive desire to be at a certain place at a certain time or as expectations that something "familiar yet unknown," will soon occur. Abductees also report feeling severe, undirected anxiety at this point even though nothing unusual has actually occurred yet. This period of foreboding can last for up to several days before the abduction actually takes place or be completely absent.

Eventually, the experiencer will undergo an apparent "shift" into an altered state of consciousness. British abduction researchers have called this change in consciousness "the Oz Factor." External sounds cease to have any significance to the experiencer and fall out of perception. They report feeling introspective and unusually calm. This stage marks a transition from normal activity to a state of "limited self-willed mobility." As consciousness shifts one or more lights are alleged to appear, occasionally accompanied by a strange mist. The source and nature of the lights differ by report; sometimes the light emanates from a source outside the house (presumably the abductors' UFO), sometimes the lights are in the bedroom with the experiencer and transform into alien figures.

As the alleged abduction proceeds, claimants say they will walk or be levitated into an alien craft, in the latter case often through solid objects such as walls, ceilings or a closed window. Alternatively, they may experience rising through a tunnel or along a beam of light, with or without the abductors accompanying them, into the awaiting craft.

Examination

The examination phase of the so-called "abduction narrative" is characterized by the performance of medical procedures and examinations by apparently alien beings against or irrespective of the will of the experiencer. Such procedures often focus on sex and reproductive biology. However, the literature holds reports of a wide variety of procedures allegedly performed by the beings. The entity that appears to be in charge of the operation is often taller than the others involved, and is sometimes described as appearing to be of a different species.

Miller notes different areas of emphasis between human medicine and what is reported as being practiced by the abductors. This could result from a difference in the purpose of the examination—routine diagnosis and/or treatment versus scientific examination of an unfamiliar species, or it could be due to a different level of technology that renders certain kinds of manual procedures unnecessary. The abductors' areas of interest appear to be the cranium (see below), nervous system, skin, reproductive system, and to a lesser degree, the joints. Systems given less attention than a human doctor would, or omitted entirely include cardiovascular system, the respiratory system below the pharynx and the lymphatic system. The abductors also appear to ignore the upper region of the abdomen in favor of the lower one. The abductors do not appear to wear gloves during the "examination." Other constants of terrestrial medicine like pills and tablets are missing from abduction narratives although sometimes abductees are asked to drink liquids. Injections also seem to be rare and IVs are almost completely absent. Dr. Miller says he's never heard an abductee claim to have a tongue depressor used on them.

Subsequent Abduction Procedures

After the so-called medical exam, the alleged abductees often report other procedures being performed with the entities. Common among these post-examination procedures are what abduction researchers refer to as imaging, envisioning, staging, and testing.

"Imaging" procedures consist of an abductee being made to view screens displaying images and scenes that appear to be specially chosen with the intent to provoke certain emotional responses in the abductee.

"Envisioning" is a similar procedure, with the primary difference being that the images being viewed, rather than being on a screen, actually seem to be projected into the experiencer's mind.

"Staging" procedures have the abductee playing a more active role, according to reports containing this element. It shares vivid hallucination-like mental visualization with the envisioning procedures, but during staging the abductee interacts with the illusionary scenario like a role player or an actor.

"Testing" marks something of a departure from the above procedures in that it lacks the emotional analysis feature. During testing the experiencer is placed in front of a complicated electronic device and is instructed to operate it. The experiencer is often confused, saying that they do not know how to operate it. However, when they actually set about performing the task, the abductee will find that they do, in fact, know how to operate the machine.

Child Presentation

Abductees of all ages and genders sometimes report being subjected to a "child presentation." As its name implies, the child presentation involves the abduction claimant being shown a "child." Often the children appear to be neither human, nor the same species as the abductors. Instead, the child will almost always share characteristics of both species. These children are labeled by experiencers as hybrids between humans and their abductors, usually Greys.

Unlike Budd Hopkins and David Jacobs, folklorist Thomas E. Bullard could not identify a child presentation phase in the abduction narrative, even after undertaking a study of 300 abduction reports. Bullard says that the child presentation "seems to be an innovation in the story" and that "no clear antecedents" to descriptions of the child presentation phase exists before its popularization by Hopkins and Jacobs.

Less Common Elements

Bullard also studied the 300 reports of alien abduction in an attempt to observe the less prominent aspects of the claims. He notes the emergence of four general categories of events that recur regularly, although not as frequently as stereotypical happenings like the medical examination. These four types of events are:

- 1.The conference
- 2.The tour
- 3.The journey
- 4.Theophany

Chronologically within abduction reports these rarer episodes tend to happen in the order listed, between the medical examination and the return.

After allegedly displaying cold callous disregard towards the abduction experiencers, sometimes the entities will change drastically in behavior once the initial medical exam is completed. They become more relaxed and hospitable towards their captive and lead him or her away from the site of the examination. The entities then hold a conference with the experiencer, wherein they discuss things relevant to the abduction phenomenon. Bullard notes five general categories of discussion that occur during the conference "phase" of reported abduction narratives: An interrogation session, explanatory segment, task assignment, warnings, and prophecies.

Tours of the abductors' craft are a rare but recurring feature of the abduction narrative. The tour seems to be given by the alleged abductors as a courtesy in response to the harshness and physical rigors of the forced medical examination. Sometimes the abductee reports traveling on a "journey" to orbit around Earth or what appears to be other planets. Some abductees find that the experience is terrifying, particularly if the aliens are of a more fearsome species, or if the abductee was subjected to extensive probing and medical testing.

Return

Eventually the abductors will return the abductees to terra firma, usually to exactly the same location and circumstances they were in before being taken. Usually, explicit memories of the abduction experience will not be present, and the abductee will only realize they have experienced "missing time" upon checking a timepiece.

Sometimes the alleged abductors appear to make mistakes when returning their captives. Famed UFO researcher Budd Hopkins has joked about "the cosmic application of Murphy's Law" in response to this observation. Hopkins has estimated that these "errors" accompany 4–5 percent of abduction reports.

One type of common apparent mistake made by the abductors is failing to return the experiencer to the same spot that they were taken from initially. This can be as simple as a different room in the same house, or abductees can even find themselves outside and all the doors of the house are locked from the inside. Another common (and amusing) error is putting the abductee's clothes (e.g. pajamas) on backwards.

Realization Event

Physician and abduction researcher John G. Miller sees significance in the reason a person would come to see themselves as being a victim of the abduction phenomenon. He terms the insight or development leading to this shift in identity from non-abductee to abductee the "realization event." The realization event is often a single, memorable experience, but Miller reports that not all abductees experience it as a distinct episode. Either way, the realization event can be thought of as the "clinical horizon" of the abduction experience.

Trauma and Recovery

Most people alleging alien abductions report invasive examinations of their bodies and some ascribe psychological trauma to their experiences. Alleged abductees claim their memories of the abduction events have caused posttraumatic stress disorder (PTSD).

"Post abduction syndrome" is a term used by abductees to describe the effects of abduction, though it is not recognized by any professional treatment organizations. The difference between PAS and PTSD is described as the recurrence of the phenomenon and the inability to identify when the disorder started; furthermore, the medical community considers PTSD to be a severe and debilitating ailment whereas "PAS" has been promoted only by fringe researchers.

Hypnosis

Many alien abductees recall much of their abduction(s) through hypnosis. Because of this, it is claimed by some skeptics that the vast majority of evidence for alien abduction is based on memories 'recovered' through hypnosis. Due to the extensive use of hypnosis, the abduction narratives are frequently explained by skeptics as false memories and suggestions by the hypnotherapist.

Argument Against the Use of Hypnosis

Alleged abductees seek out hypnotherapists to try to resolve issues such as missing time or unexplained physical symptoms such as muscle pain or headaches. This usually involves two phases, an information gathering stage, in which the hypnotherapist asks about unexplained illnesses or unusual phenomena during the patients' lives (caused by or distortions of the alleged abduction), followed by hypnosis and guided imagery to facilitate recall. The information gathering enhances the likelihood that the events discussed will be incorporated into later abduction "memories".

Seven steps are hypothesized to lead to the development of false memories:

- 1. A person is predisposed to accept the idea that certain puzzling or inexplicable experiences might be telltale signs of UFO abduction.

- 2. The person seeks out a therapist, whom he or she views as an authority and who is, at the very least, receptive to this explanation and has some prior familiarity with UFO abduction reports.

- 3. Alternatively, the therapist frames the puzzling experiences in terms of an abduction narrative.

- 4. Alternative explanations of the experiences are not explored.
- 5. There is increasing commitment to the abduction explanation and increasing anxiety reduction associated with ambiguity reduction.
- 6. The therapist legitimates or ratifies the abductee's experience, which constitutes additional positive reinforcement.
- 7. The client adopts the role of the "victim" or abductee, which becomes integrated into the psychotherapy and the client's view of self.

Argument For the Use of Hypnosis

Harvard psychiatrist John E. Mack counters this argument, noting "It might be useful to restate that a large proportion of the material relating to abductions is recalled without the use of an altered state of consciousness, and that many abduction reporters appear to relive powerful experiences after only the most minimal relaxation exercise, hardly justifying the word hypnosis at all. The relaxation exercise is useful to relieve the experiencer's need to attend to the social demands and other stimuli of face-to-face conversation, and to relieve the energies involved in repressing memories and emotion."

Perspectives

There have been a variety of explanations offered for abduction phenomena, ranging from sharply skeptical appraisals, to uncritical acceptance of all abductee claims, to the demonological, to everything in between.

Some have elected not to try explaining things, instead noting similarities to other phenomena, or simply documenting the development of the alien abduction phenomenon.

Others are intrigued by the entire phenomenon, but hesitate in making any definitive conclusions. The late Harvard psychiatrist John E. Mack concluded, "The furthest you can go at this point is to say there's an authentic mystery here. And that is, I think, as far as anyone ought to go."

Putting aside the question of whether abduction reports are literally and objectively "real", literature professor Terry Matheson argues that their popularity and their intriguing appeal are easily understood. Tales of abduction "are intrinsically absorbing; it is hard to imagine a more vivid description of human powerlessness." After experiencing the frisson of delightful terror one may feel from reading ghost stories or watching horror movies, Matheson notes that people "can return to the safe world of their homes, secure in the knowledge that the phenomenon in question cannot follow. But as the abduction myth has stated almost from the outset, there is no avoiding alien abductors."

Matheson writes that when compared to the earlier contactee reports, abduction accounts are distinguished by their "relative sophistication and subtlety, which enabled them to enjoy an immediately more favorable reception from the public."

Attempts at Confirmation

It has been argued that if actual "flesh and blood" aliens are abducting humans, there should be some hard evidence that this is occurring. Proponents of the physical reality of the abduction experience have suggested ways that could conceivably confirm abduction reports.

One procedure reported occurring during the alleged exam phase of the experience is the insertion of a long needle-like contraption into a woman's navel. Some have speculated that this could be a form of laparoscopy. If this is true, after the abduction there should be free gas in the female's abdomen, which could be seen on an x-ray. The presence of free gas would be extremely abnormal, and would help substantiate the claim of some sort of procedure being done to her.

Notable abduction claims

- 1956: Elizabeth Klarer (South Africa)
- 1957: Antonio Vilas Boas (Brazil)
- 1961: Betty and Barney Hill abduction (USA)[6]
- 1967: Schirmer Abduction (USA)
- 1973: Pascagoula Abduction (USA)
- 1975: Travis Walton (USA)
- 1976: Allagash Abductions (USA)
- 1978: Valentich disappearance (Australia)
- 1979: Robert Taylor incident (Scotland)
- 1970s–1980s: Whitley Strieber (USA)
- 1990: Danielle Egnew (USA)
- 1994: Meng Zhaoguo incident (China)
- 1997: Kirsan Ilyumzhinov (Russia)[40]

EPILOGE

After reading the material in this book, it should become clear that there are more things in the world than we can understand. There are many things that go bump in the night of which we have no understanding.

Whether it is a vampire, a werewolf, shadow people or aliens wandering into your bedroom in the middle of the night, our homes are not the proverbial castle. At any moment our world can be invaded by something from the otherwhere.

INDEX

CPSIA information can be obtained
at www.ICGtesting.com
Printed in the USA
FSOW03n2344241016
26532FS